Inland
Cruising Companion

Also by John Liley

Journeys of the Swan
France – the Quiet Way

Inland
Cruising Companion

John Liley

STANFORD MARITIME   LONDON

Stanford Maritime Limited
Member Company of the George Philip Group
12 Long Acre   London WC2E 9LP

First published in Great Britain 1977
Copyright © John Liley 1977

Set in 11/12 pt Monophoto Baskerville
Printed in Great Britain by Butler & Tanner Ltd
Frome and London

ISBN 0 540 07167 6

Jacket photo of the Caledonian Canal by
Leslie Bryce, courtesy of British Waterways Board

Contents

Acknowledgements

Much of the information in this book was gathered while working for *Waterways World*, *Practical Boat Owner*, and *Motor Boat and Yachting*, and I am grateful to the Editors and staff of all three for the facilities that they have provided. I would also like to thank Nigel Warren for permission to reproduce a portion of his propeller tables, first published in *Practical Boat Owner*; and Dick Everitt, of the same magazine, for undertaking all the drawing work in these pages.

J.N.L.

Introducing Waterways

Whether the wheel was invented before the raft is uncertain, but inland waterways have been in use for a very long time. The marine engine keeps the present day voyager from hoisting sail in a world of low bridges and sharp corners, nor need he wrestle with some dark-spirited horse; but it is the connection with the past that makes so many waterways attractive.

Those in Britain are a monument to the Industrial Revolution. Once, gangs of men would tow small vessels against the current of some fast-flowing river, perhaps using weirs to restrain the water and improve the depth. Passage beyond each weir would be through a gate, or by removing planks, and the levels were crudely adjusted, with frequent differences of opinion. Nowadays a lock will do the same job, with a weir alongside to accommodate the flow, and entirely natural navigations have become rare. Some navigable rivers still flow unhindered through the Norfolk Broads, but the change in level is small and their course is relatively placid. On other English rivers, most notably the Thames, Nene, Trent and Severn, there are frequent locks, and sections of canal to replace some of the awkward portions. Only the lowest reaches remain in anything like the natural state, and here the tide takes charge. Early craft floated up with the flood tide and descended on the ebb, and even with a powerful engine it pays to do the same.

Canals form a large part of the English system. Many cross a watershed, linking one valley with the next, and in addition to the locks, which occur, on average, about once every mile, there are occasional tunnels and aqueducts. These canals connect with many rivers, but only craft under 7 ft in beam can make the journey from the north to the south of England by an inland route. The origins of this tiny dimension are lost in

A narrow lock on the Oxford Canal, 7 ft wide and typical of the English Midlands.

the fog of history, but it remains as the width of a lock on the 'narrow' canals. In length each lock is slightly greater than 70 ft overall, and the theoretical depth of these canals is 3 ft or 3 ft 6 in, depending upon the ambitions of the constructors. In reality, many of these waterways are badly silted, and it is fashionable now to speak of 2 ft as a reasonable draft. Boats drawing up to 3 ft can get through with frequent groundings, and thereafter progress becomes impossible.

The 'broad' waterways of England are fractionally deeper, and many have locks of 70 ft by 14 ft, or over. Inevitably there are exceptions, such as the Leeds & Liverpool Canal, which only takes boats up to 62 ft, and several waterways in Yorkshire, with locks down to 57 ft overall. Short locks are also to be found in Fenland, and of less than 14 ft in width on the River Stort, the Wey, and portions of the Kennet & Avon Canal. Precise details are given in many of the gazetteers now available.

Several waterways are not connected to this central network. Among them are the popular and easily navigable Norfolk Broads, and the Brecon & Abergavenny Canal. The Caledonian Canal provides a chain of lakes and locked connections right across Scotland and incorporates Loch Ness, while in Ireland there are several river and lake systems. The Grand Canal connects the River Shannon and Dublin, and there is an arm to the River Barrow in the south.

8

The facilities

With the growth of pleasure cruising in Britain, facilities for hiring, maintenance and repair are now extensive, although the centres of the cities provide an ironical exception. A further curiosity is the heavy pressure upon permanent moorings in the countryside and their absence in the towns, where docks and arms have been habitually closed and filled in. The casual traveller will have little difficulty in mooring overnight, but it must be stressed that for what in Britain are regarded as 'large' vessels, a permanent base can be difficult to find. Houseboat moorings are at a premium anywhere, because of the paranoid objection to them by local authorities.

Boat licences are required to navigate most British rivers and canals, with charges based upon the size of craft. A variety of regulations and conventions apply. To date, however, no 'driving licence' is required upon British waterways – a measure of independence that many boat-owners cherish.

The administration of British waterways has long been complex, and reflects the lack of interest of successive governments. Nationalization in 1948 was half-hearted; some waterways stayed in the hands of private companies, while others, principally rivers, have been administered by water authorities. Several more have had to be rescued by voluntary trusts.

A further attempt is now being made to reorganize, and a recommended source of reference is the Inland Waterways Association of 114 Regent's Park Road, London NW1. This voluntary body has for many years challenged the unsatisfactory standing of waterways in British society, and without it a large number would have ceased as navigations. The Association welcomes new members, and can also provide details of smaller organizations devoted to individual waterways, as well as voluntary working party groups which throughout the year work on restoration projects.

Progress

High speed travel and the motorway have conditioned many of us to covering large distances in a single day; but on a river or canal 20 miles is a long way, and often the total daily run.

The Upper Thames, a wide waterway where locks are worked by keepers.

In planning a route, points to bear in mind are the low average travelling speed, and the time spent in locks. Speed limits on canals are usually 4 mph, and on many rivers 6 mph, but there are frequent occasions when it is prudent to go much slower, and anyone travelling at speed will make few friends in the course of the voyage. Respectable averages are 3–4 mph, with say ten minutes at each lock on a narrow canal, fifteen minutes for a broad one, and rather more on a river, where locks will normally be worked by keepers. On the Thames, for example, the professional keepers often have to shepherd many craft at a time, and half an hour per lock is not an unreasonable estimate for a busy period.

The terminology

Though archaic, maritime terminology is absolutely unambiguous. The port side is the left-hand side of a vessel when you are standing aboard her and looking forward (towards the front). The word 'port' has the same number of letters as 'left' and the system may be loosely remembered in this way; the other side being 'starboard'.

Inland waterways also have words of their own, many of them perpetuated because of quaintness or, one suspects, their failure to enter the *Oxford English Dictionary*; but to the horror of the nautical purist 'left' and 'right' are often used for 'port' and 'starboard', as well as 'back' and 'front' instead of 'stern' and 'bow'. 'Reverse' is also used for 'going astern', perhaps because the canals centre on the English Midlands, where the influence of the motor car is well known. The enthusiast may also speak of 'strap' for 'rope' or 'fan' for 'propeller', occasionally deviating into semi-nautical words such as 'starn' (so pronounced by Nelson, because of a nasal defect).

None of this does much harm, save during a hiatus, when a left/right mix-up could be disastrous. As far as possible, waterway terminology has been used in the remainder of this book, but where it is important, 'port' and 'starboard' are employed as well.

Some Traditional Craft

In theory any boat might be used on rivers and canals, provided she can fit the locks and squeeze through the bridges; but some are better than others. It must be remembered throughout that all boats represent a compromise of some kind. A bad boat for inland waterways may be a good one at sea, and *vice versa*; a big one is roomy, but costs more to run, while a small vessel, though cheap, versatile and easy to tow behind a car, may be cramped and squalid when afloat. When people ask for advice on buying or hiring a boat, the hardest problem by far is to identify the type of boating they will really be able to do, and to separate reality from the nebulae of myth, dreams and totally impossible requirements.

It is often instructive to consider traditional or regional craft, and a fair number of these are to be found on the English system. They demonstrate several basic points.

The 70 ft unpowered 'narrow boat' is symbolic of the English Midland canals and it was for this vessel that many of the locks were built. When loaded, such a boat would carry 25 or 30 tons of cargo, with the crew, often a family, housed in the tiny rear cabin. Towing was by a single horse, which found such work comparatively little effort, and surprising speed would be achieved. In later years the majority of these craft survived as 'butties' or towed craft, working in pairs with motor narrow

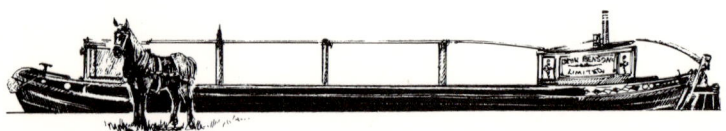

The traditional craft of the English canals, the 70 ft 'narrow boat'.

boats. Goods carrying has now almost ceased on the English canals, but several of these boats remain in original condition, or converted with a cabin over the hold.

The advantages of unpowered boats are their glorious smoothness and silence under tow, but they require considerable skill and the dextrous use of ropes at locks. With the disappearance of the towpath on certain canals, coupled with the remonstrances of dozing bystanders and disapproving frowns from the authorities, horse towing has become harder over the years, and is nowadays confined to specialized day-trip boats. Other unpowered boats work in the company of a motor boat, often as 'hotel boats', and this necessitates double working at many of the locks.

The narrow boat type demonstrates flared bows and curved stem, designed to rub against a lock gate without catching on it. The inward slope of the cabin keeps it clear of bridge and tunnel walls and the heavy wooden rudder, which is necessary in the absence of the push from a propeller, is designed to fold tightly across if needs be, with the tiller withdrawn from its socket. The hull is designed to fill a narrow lock to the maximum, and is tough enough to pass through without fenders. Traditional construction is in timber, but many of the boats built in the 1930s are of 'composite' construction, with the wooden bottom planks bolted to upright steel sides.

Though embodying much of the spirit of the canals, these craft have often deteriorated with age, and they can be difficult to convert to power. Outboard conversions are generally gimcrack, while installing an inboard unit involves a complete rebuild at the back end. Occasionally old narrow boats have been shortened, either by eliminating a centre section, or by abruptly sawing in two and inserting a transom. In some cases butties have been converted into two boats, the old stern becoming a new bow. Provided that the work is sound there is no reason to deride the practice, and a number of serviceable boats have been so produced.

The motor narrow boat is a broadly similar type, but has a different stern, built to take a propeller from the outset, with the engine usually housed forward of the crew's quarters and the shaft passing under the cabin floor. Hundreds of these boats were built, the majority during the 1930s, and many remain,

Motor narrow boats are more common. Many have been converted, as here, with a cabin over the hold.

either unconverted or with a long cabin added. Contrary to first impressions, they can be a joy to handle, steering with great precision, provided that the water is deep enough; but the greater draft at the stern makes for slow progress in a shallow canal, and many have worn heavily on the bottom.

The criteria of unpowered narrow boats apply here, and the traditional engine should also be treated with scepticism, for many of these have become badly worn and therefore temperamental. For years the single cylinder Bolinder semi-diesel was the mainstay of English canal traffic, a tough, crude engine that could run day and night. Starting was by blowlamp, and the total loss lubrication tended to shower the vicinity with soots. Some had gearboxes; others went astern by stalling and then opening up again on the reverse stroke. Such engines, producing an unforgettable exhaust note, heavy-laden with nostalgia, are for the real canal enthusiast, but he needs to be an engineering enthusiast as well.

Barges come in many shapes and sizes. The term normally refers to vessels of twice the width of a narrow boat or over (it being *infra dig* to refer to a narrow boat as a 'barge'). Two traditional barges shown here are a Yorkshire 'keel' of about 60 tons capacity, a regional type that provides handsome living accommodation when converted; and a Dutch sailing barge, the only vessel of those so far considered that is at all suitable for open

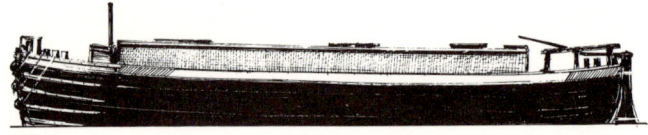

A barge is a bigger vessel, generally about 14 ft in beam, or over. The type shown here, a Yorkshire keel, offers ample space for living aboard.

14

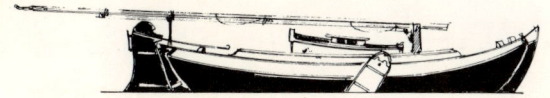

A Dutch type, a boeier. Traditional Dutch sailing craft, once used for fishing or for general cargoes, are still being built as yachts. The design combines reasonable seaworthiness with sufficient sturdiness for inland waterways.

waters or the sea. This latter type sails with the aid of leeboards mounted on the sides, and these may be lowered to act in the same manner as a keel or centreplate. Properly trimmed and ballasted, and in competent hands, such craft sail well enough. Mast lowering gear and a sturdy engine make them reasonably suitable for rivers and wide canals; but several projections demand careful moving in the locks.

On the Continent, wear and tear is less, primarily because the waterways are deep and in better order, while traditions of barge maintenance and upkeep have remained very high. It is not uncommon to find barges dating back to the 1890s in first class condition. In Britain the handling has been rougher, particularly during the later days of trade, and many barges are badly knocked about. All that has been inferred about narrow boats applies once again, and there is the added difficulty of finding waterways big enough to accommodate these craft. There is also a temptation to take them to sea, and though a number have made such trips they are not really suitable. The high sides are vulnerable to wind, the bluff bow can be stopped by waves, the propeller is too near the surface and the rudder is too exposed. Judicious ballasting might make things better, provided that the hull is sound, but such a trip comes into the fear and trepidation category and cannot be formally recommended. Needless to say, narrow boats embody all these disadvantages and more, including instability in waves, and London on a fine day represents their limit.

Modern Boats

Four typical boats may be considered next: a modern steel-hulled cruiser built on 'narrow boat' lines, a fibreglass (GRP) cruiser of a type common in estuaries and coastal waters, a smaller version of the same thing but specifically built for inland use, and a large flat-bottomed type often found in hire fleets on wider waterways. For the sake of illustration, these boats have been fitted with, respectively, a diesel inboard engine, a petrol inboard driving through an inboard/outboard unit, or 'outdrive' leg, an outboard motor, and a diesel with hydraulic transmission.

The steel-hulled canal cruiser

These boats have evolved in recent years and are similar in many respects to the traditional motor narrow boat. They lack the history, but also the wear and tear that time can bestow. More particularly, they lack the narrow boat's embarrassing draft. A modern steel-hulled cruiser will draw no more than 2 ft and measure 6 ft 10 in in beam. Lengths vary up to the traditional 70 ft, and construction is generally in mild steel plate with internal reinforcement.

The steel-hulled canal cruiser, displaying many of the same characteristics as the motor narrow boat, save in draft, which is usually under 2 ft.

The cabin sides and roof may also be in steel, usually in a thinner gauge to maintain stability, but they are commonly built in fibreglass or timber. Superficial, but nonetheless important, points to check are that the hull is well equipped with rubbing strips to take the wear in locks, that the bow will not catch on gates, that the cabin top slopes inward for bridges and is strong enough to withstand elephantine figures descending from a lockside.

Handrails should be firm and either welded or bolted through the roof with timber reinforcement pads. Likewise all bollards must be substantial and of a type that can hold a rope extending upwards. Ease of stepping on and off at bow and stern is most important, since this will be done at every lock. There should also be a means of walking from bow to stern outside the boat, either over the cabin roof, or by edging along the hull side on a ledge provided for that purpose. Some users frown on this practice, and it is true that it has its dangers, mainly through over-familiarity; but if the ledge is to be used, it should be wide and flat, and not too slippery when wet.

The bottled gas installation must also be outside and in a vented container. The popular place nowadays is in the bow, and sometimes the bottles protrude so that they catch ropes, or can leak gas into the rest of the boat. The vents ought to be at the container bottom, leading outside the hull, as gas flows downwards.

The commonest arrangement of cabins is with a central gangway passing through them all, with the saloon and galley combined at the forward end. Access to the outside world in either direction is an important safety point in any boat.

Galley equipment comes close to the household type, save that refrigerators, generally working on gas, are smaller and lighter than in the home. Water heating is often by gas also, with a wall type heater unit, but elaborate liquid fuel systems are also available.

Cabin walls and roofs are normally lined, either with laminate or timber, to defeat condensation. Headroom varies, but 6 ft, at least, is obtainable and some boats manage 6 ft 4 in on the centreline. Personal taste aside, interiors should have bunks that are long and wide; 5 ft 11 in by 1 ft 11 in is common, but not enough for everybody, and some builders manage much

Typical interior of a steel-hulled canal boat. The galley is in the saloon, and the bench seat can be rearranged to form a double berth. A lavatory compartment lies behind the partition in the background, and beyond that is another sleeping cabin. Many fittings, such as the water heater on the wall, calorific gas heater behind the table, and the small refrigerator, are virtually standard on such boats. TV is an 'extra' (one that not all waterway devotees approve).

more, with good stowage space and reasonable privacy. In this latter respect, the lavatory can often be criticized, being central, far from soundproof, and sometimes ventilating into adjacent cabins. Locating it at the back end has its advantages. Showers are frequently installed and tend to be rather cramped; notwithstanding, one great virtue of this type of vessel is the space that she affords within the clearances of a narrow canal.

The steering position may be in a large rear cockpit, with either a stool, a wide rail (sometimes passing within a finger's width of the wall of a lock) or nothing at all, when the steerer will have to stand at the tiller. Alternatives are a traditional hatchway, which compels friends and family to cling like limpets to the outside in order to keep company; or wheel steering located elsewhere. The disadvantage of wheel steering is that it affords nothing like the precision in handling vessels of this type, and if located forward it is difficult to see all that is happening while entering or working through a lock.

The details of engine installation are given in another chapter. Suffice to say here that it should be workmanlike and tidy. An enclosed engineroom affords advantages in comfort while working but is wasteful of space, and a common approach is to put the engine beneath the cockpit floor, where, if anything, it is more accessible.

The great majority of these craft are fitted with 'marine' diesel engines, in practice often adapted industrial or motor vehicle units, suitably marinized with different cooling and transmission systems. With proper installation and maintenance these engines are highly reliable, long-lived and safe, with neither the fire risk nor the running expense of a petrol engine. Their disadvantages are higher initial cost and greater vibration. The greater weight of a diesel is not a disadvantage, since ballast often has to be added anyway. Some air-cooled diesels are noisy, and several water cooled units no less so. In practice, noise insulation is difficult to achieve, and much depends upon the structure of the motor itself. Marine gearboxes are sometimes also noisy; if buying, a few preliminary checks on other boats may pay dividends. A further consideration with gearboxes is the use of a hydraulic gear-change mechanism, worked by a pump and valve system. Though more complex, and occasionally given to failure on its own, this device permits gear-changing without stress, whereas a 'manual' change, with the lever directly connected, can have dire effects in the hands of the ham-fisted. With a lock every mile, and perhaps a dozen gear changes at every lock, the point is important. Hydraulic gear-changes can also be positioned more flexibly in the boat.

To sum up: these can be excellent boats for the narrow canals, tough, practical and roomy for the limits imposed. They are also quite rewarding to handle – provided that tiller steering is used (and the helmsman doesn't mind the rain). They are less suitable for wider waterways, particularly where wash or waves are of any consequence, and dangerous in estuaries. They would also fare badly on the Continent owing to heavy wash on many of the larger rivers and canals.

The fast fibreglass motor cruiser

Here we enter difficult territory, for a boat of this type is more vulnerable. Fibreglass (GRP) does not react too kindly to abrasion and the hull will need protection in the locks. Portable fenders may do the trick, but they have an irritating habit of being swept aside at the *moment juste*, or of catching behind a gate when entering. If she is of a seagoing type, she will have a flared bow to prevent her from digging into waves, and this can also cause problems as it overhangs the lockside.

These cruisers are comparatively light for their size, and often quite difficult to handle at close quarters. They can be vulnerable to wind and sometimes, but not always, tippy with the movement of the crew. Other points to check are ease of access to deck and interior from the cockpit (sometimes rather an obstacle race), and sensible cleats and fittings, which should be firmly bolted through both the deck and timber reinforcement pads beneath. Cleats and fairleads commonly found on small cruisers often are undersized, and not effective when lines lead upwards, to a lockside.

With an 'outdrive', steering is from a wheel which turns the entire underwater part of the unit, and a different technique is necessary, since there is little rudder effect with the power shut off. The temptation is to proceed in a series of high speed

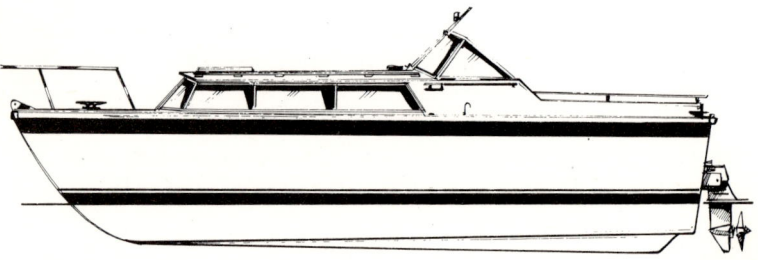

A modern motor cruiser, suitable for open waters but vulnerable against lock sides and walls. An 'outdrive' transmission is shown here.

jerks, but with practice and a calm temperament these units are quite manageable at low speeds, and even offer certain advantages in going astern or in lifting the propeller from the water. Generally, however, they are vulnerable in tight surroundings, being less well protected than the propeller of a conventional 'inboard' installation.

On the other hand, such a boat is much better suited to lakes and to open water, in which the narrow boat can hardly survive at all, and provided that she has decent beam and a good engine allied to sound construction she will be far more versatile. She might even be of the 'planing' type, capable of high speeds by virtue of partially rising from the water, and on Loch Ness and kindred thoroughfares she will come into her own. Needless to say, this speed is of no benefit in confined waters, unless aggravation and lawsuits are the aim.

Internally, much depends upon size. Headroom is sometimes tight, and quite elaborate linings are often necessary to thwart condensation. A common furnishing arrangement is the 'dinette', in which the table can be lowered to fill the gap between bench seating and thus provide a double bed; and there are often tapering bunks in the bow which can likewise be linked to form a double, usually by inserting a triangular piece of upholstery. If these two sleeping areas are located in the same cabin, there is little in the way of privacy, and a mere curtain may be all that separates them. Bigger boats have a timber bulkhead in between, while a centre cockpit offers a more satisfactory division, if greater difficulty in steering. Occasionally, and particularly if the boat is Scandinavian in origin, the stove is in the cockpit, with a complicated arrangement of tables and folding seats. This necessitates a major upheaval every time the kettle is put on, but wins some valuable space, and can be quite civilized with the awning up, in summer.

Further space has been saved by the use of the 'outdrive', and this is one of its great advantages, coupled with comparative ease of installation. The disadvantage of all petrol engines is their heavy fuel consumption and the fire risk, which is greater than in a car, owing to the enclosing nature of the hull. For these reasons, petrol has fallen into disrepute in marine circles, save in high performance craft or those fitted with outboards.

21

Diesel outdrives are available, including some rather cumbersome single cylinder units, but the heavy vibration at low speed requires really substantial mounting on proper bearers rather than simply bolting through the transom.

To sum up: horses are for courses; such cruisers are better suited to big lakes, estuaries, or – subject to all the usual provisos – the open sea. They are comparatively awkward inland, may be over-powered, and require some care and skill in handling.

Small fibreglass cruisers for inland waterways

Several of the same criticisms apply, but with thoughtful design quite serviceable craft can be provided for canal and river use. Protection against rubbing is important, and this is often achieved by having longitudinal timber strips on the outside of the hull, sometimes with wooden pads to take the impact when the stern swings against a wall. If seagoing is forgotten, upright lines may be featured and these make working through the locks a little easier, as well as providing greater space inside. Well designed boats have easy access onto the side decks and substantial, firmly bolted fittings. Rails should not project, and there must also be a hatch in the foredeck, or some other escape route, in case of emergency.

The dinette and tapered bow bunk arrangement is common, with a lavatory compartment, often rather a cramped one, located near the door out into the cockpit. Full standing headroom is usually difficult to achieve, because of low bridge clearances and the fact that such boats float high in the water. Windscreens and cockpit awnings become vulnerable, and are often designed to fold flat.

There are mixed views on outboards, which are convenient but comparatively expensive to run, with a certain fire risk,

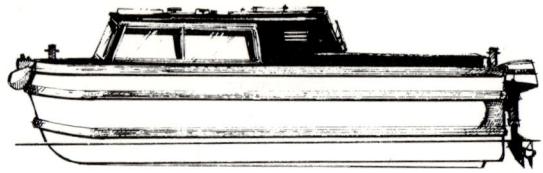

A small motor cruiser with heavy rubbing strakes for inland waters.

high noise level and the same difficulty in handling at very low speeds as with an outdrive. Almost without exception they work on the simpler, less efficient two-stroke cycle and they are more temperamental.

Several of these problems derive from over-powering, the commonest fault on inland waterways today. While it is true that a reserve of power is useful in a wind, or for a rare river in flood, the amount needed to propel a boat on still waters is astonishingly small. A large motor running virtually at tick-over will consume more fuel than a small one working hard; it will also be more prone to failure, and if an electric charging unit is fitted it may not reach the speeds at which it will give net current. A motor of the correct power output, properly maintained and not tampered with, should give reasonable service. For craft up to 20 ft long 6 hp is adequate, and for 25-footers a nominal 10 hp is quite enough. Beyond these sizes an inboard installation should be seriously considered.

Interior of a 24 ft fibreglass cruiser. The small table may be removed and the seats on either side used as bunks. The seat in the foreground also forms part of a double berth, and the curtains on either side may be pulled across the cabin to give a measure of privacy.

Wide-beamed cruisers

Larger motor cruisers are popular on the Thames and some of the Fenland waterways which allow greater space, and where lock working is not particularly onerous. They have become almost traditional on the Norfolk Broads, where there are effectively no locks at all. For many years these boats were built of timber, often to a very high standard, using established yacht construction techniques. Latterly they have been in fibreglass, but few of the disadvantages touched upon have the same importance in clearer waters. The greater beam allows more interior and deck space, and a reliable inboard engine. A centre cockpit becomes practicable, often with a sliding top (if sleeping under one of these, incidentally, it will be found to be far from draught-free).

A modification of the type has appeared in great quantity in recent years, moulded in fibreglass and with some quite sensible adaptations for working through locks. Such boats are almost rectangular in plan, with straight sides that are heavily protected with rubbing rails. Steering is from an enclosed position within the saloon at the forward end, and the power unit, a diesel, is mounted compactly in the stern, with hydraulic transmission to the propeller. Such a vessel is virtually a floating flat, the layout permitting large rectangular cabins with many comforts, plus wide side decks, a bow cockpit and a spacious roof, with a sliding sun aperture.

The type is unsuitable for estuary or sea, but has been in use for several years on Continental waterways, where they have

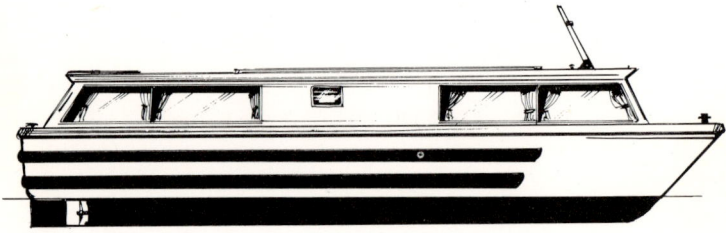

Larger inland cruisers often have an interior steering position in the main saloon, up forward. This particular type has evolved in recent years for use on the Thames, Broads, Fenland rivers and Continental canals.

24

proved both comfortable and tough. The only serious disadvantage in canals is the danger of steering from the forward end, where it is difficult to gauge the swing of the stern or check the safety of crew members in a lock. For this reason, at least one owner has fitted an alternative outside steering position, right over the stern.

Hydraulic transmission, though outwardly most attractive, poses a number of difficult questions. In principle the engine can be installed anywhere, as it drives a pump that circulates hydraulic fluid through flexible pipes. This in turn actuates the propeller, and valves permit the transmission to be reversed, or by-passed. There are various types on the market, some of astounding sophistication, but all operate on very fine tolerances, and absolute cleanliness of the fluid is essential. There are also heavy losses through the generation of heat in the high pressure piping, and cooling systems are required.

As with many specialized systems – like the 'water jet' in which the engine drives an impeller, housed in a tunnel – the individual owner may question the reliability of such a mysterious device, and more often opts for some system that is widely understood, and for which attention is easily obtainable. Despite its popularity in hire fleets, hydraulic transmission has yet to overcome these suspicions in the private owner.

Further points

Twin-screw craft, though common at sea, and more reliable thereupon, are at a disadvantage on inland routes. Even deep waterways shelve towards the bank, and the nearer propeller is vulnerable, particularly when mooring, or when meeting and passing other craft.

Sailing boats have obvious disadvantages. The mast, when lowered, often projects embarrassingly, and presents an obstacle on deck. The hull, being rounded and often not designed to rub against anything, requires heavy fendering. Old motor tyres, or even hay bales, are used to give protection.

Small boats such as canoes, skiffs, camping punts and inflatable dinghies all have their advantages and drawbacks; those who have canoed through Birmingham will know the merits of not having to pitch a tent. Paddling or rowing on canals can be dull and unrewarding by contrast with the upper reaches of some fast-flowing river. Camping punts and similar craft, though vulnerable to wind, have the merits of cheapness and transportability, and offer much pleasure to those who avoid the more wash-ridden spots and are prepared to take their time. Inflatable dinghies are superficially attractive, but tend to ship water easily and are smitten by wind. They also generate a disproportionate amount of wash, and are regarded with distrust by several waterways authorities.

Some very general principles

In choosing any boat, it pays to adopt a temporary posture of cynicism. What will she be like on a rainy day, moored outside the gasworks? Will you honestly need all that power? Do you really believe that you might also like to go to sea some day; or is this wishful thinking, imposing an unsatisfactory compromise?

Nor should a purchaser, or hirer, be afraid to ask un-nautical questions. Can you see out when sitting down? (Usually, no.) Are all bunks as cramped as this? (Again, no.) Need the lavatory be so tiny/mysterious/complicated? (Often, yes, thanks to legislation compelling that waste be pumped out/dumped ashore.)

At the same time, the mumbo-jumbo of the motor car is best forgotten. It has no place on the water, where 'streamlining' or 'styling' can be absurd, and 'dash' often seems rather sad. Likewise, many experienced users avoid the temptation to be 'yachty' which, if it has a place at all, is not on the inland waterways. Practicality is always the first priority.

26

Basic Boat Handling

Managing a boat is a vague science. No-one is totally its master, and even the experts blunder. If one thing marks the experienced boat handler, it is a sense of caution when he or she first takes control.

The controls themselves are usually simple: a wheel or tiller for steering, a throttle and a gear lever. Wheels vary between the type that decorates country restaurants and something the size of a large drawing pin, and some take more winding than

A typical single-lever throttle and gear-change control. Pushing it forward makes the boat go faster in forward gear, pulling it back engages reverse. The upright position is neutral or idling, although devices such as a release button are often fitted to enable the engine to be speeded up without putting it into gear.

others, but their function is simply to turn the boat. The tiller, though primitive, is the more precise means of handling small vessels. It is astonishing how, with practice, it becomes possible to feel a boat's movement, and to correct it, by the simple expedient of pulling or pushing on a tiller.

On a boat there are three gears only – forward, 'neutral' and reverse. The throttle is often combined with the gear-change in a single lever which works a cable. The central position will be 'neutral', when the propeller is effectively disconnected from the engine. Pushing the lever forward makes the boat go faster in forward gear; pulling it back does the same in 'reverse', or when 'going astern'.

Whatever the appearance of the control area, and the recent tendency to sprinkle it with gauges, cigar lighters and other manifestations of the 'dashboard', there are few similarities with operating a car. It is wisest to forget them.

A checklist before starting

In tackling any new boat, a pre-starting routine is called for, before switching on the engine:

1. Inspect the engine oil level (and repeat daily).
2. Check the gearbox oil level, if separate from the engine's supply (daily).

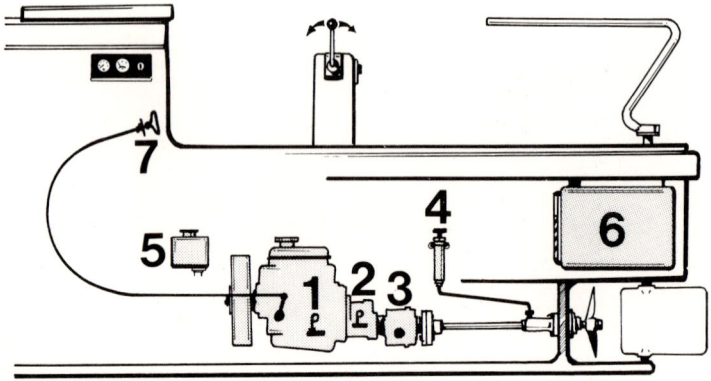

Checkpoints before starting: *1* engine oil level; *2* gearbox oil level; *3* reduction box level; *4* sterntube greaser; *5* engine water; *6* fuel; *7* engine stop control.

3. Check the reduction gearbox, if any, for oil (weekly, unless there are outside traces of loss, in which case daily).
4. Screw down the stern tube greaser (daily – a single turn of the cap is usually sufficient).
5. Inspect the cooling water level (daily, if any – some engines are air-cooled). Water inlet filters, if any, should be kept free of leaves or other debris (daily).
6. Check fuel levels (daily).
7. Sort out the control system and locate the horn. Also find a means of stopping the engine – the ignition key for petrol units, a pull-out lever or button for diesels, often mounted on a cable and secreted in some inaccessible corner.

Basic handling

Early handling experiments should be in the art of stopping. A boat has no 'brakes' in the conventional sense, and relies upon putting the engine into reverse gear, or on finding room to glide to a halt. The time taken in either case may cause an uncomfortable surprise.

Having warmed up the engine and selected a patch of water,

Tiller steering is the most effective for narrow waterways. This particular boat has a separate gear lever, by the steerer's foot.

the boat may be gingerly edged towards it. With small craft this can be done by pushing away from the bank with hands, feet or – with care and provided that nobody else's property is involved – by using the boathook. Once clear of the towpath edge and any surrounding mariners, the engine may be put into forward gear. A marine gearbox likes a little time to think about things, so a second or two back in 'neutral' is advisable before engaging reverse gear. Frequently nothing happens at all, and increased engine speed is necessary to slow the boat down.

These early experiments allow some estimate of a boat's momentum, and any tendency to rotate. On all craft with a single fixed propeller there is a possibility that the vessel may turn when she goes astern. The phenomenon, known as 'paddle-wheel effect', varies from boat to boat, from the negligible to the extremely alarming. The causes are rooted in the dynamics of propeller design, and to a certain extent in hull form. In serious cases it demands precise judgement, but such

A small boat moving cautiously on a river, with just sufficient speed or 'way' to maintain control. (Robert Shopland, *Waterways World*)

vessels are fortunately rare. With outboard or 'outdrive' units the effect is over-ridden in steering.

Once confidence has been gained a slightly firmer approach will pay dividends, but the commonest mistakes in boat handling are travelling too fast and revving the engine excessively. As a general rule, it is good practice to slow down early, putting the engine in 'neutral' with time to spare, and gliding to a halt. A brief touch forward will take the boat on again, if required, while sharp alterations in course can be made at low speed by putting the rudder well over then giving a brief burst of power. In general, boats pivot on a point somewhere between one-third and one-half of their length back from the bow, and at speed some tend to slide sideways on a turn.

These techniques are used to perfection by Continental barge-masters, who are never afraid to slow down early, despite the fact that time is money. They are always willing to take their time in a tight spot, and the care with which craft are handled, even when others are waiting, provides an object lesson in self-control.

Handling becomes harder in a wind, and anticipation remains important. In a cross wind, the boat will have to be headed into it slightly. With a head wind she may have to be kicked round with a brief burst of power from time to time, if, say, waiting for a lock. When the wind is behind, she will have to be slowed down earlier, and always with a clear space ahead. It is here that an understanding of the 'paddle-wheel effect' pays dividends, as there may be no alternative to going hard astern. Ideally the boat should have been set swinging in a contrary direction first – a manœuvre that is easier said than done.

On a river it is essential to turn the boat to face upstream into the current before attempting to moor to the bank. Before making the turn it is well to look over the shoulder first, in case some other vessel is passing, when you may have to wait. Once headed into the stream the boat may be held against it on the engine, and then cautiously manœuvred across. The only exception will be when waiting at a lock, where the current will generally be slack anyway. If wind and current are in different directions, a brief trial in clear water will give a good indication of how the boat will behave. Movement can usually be checked by sighting against objects on the bank.

The perils of wash. A cruiser passes too fast on a Fenland river, and the moored boats are about to feel the effects. The farther two may well bang together.

Three useful general rules in boat handling are:

1. Always slow down in good time, and at the first hint of trouble.
2. Rely upon going astern as little as possible.
3. Face the boat into any strong current before coming alongside.

The channel

With some rare exceptions, waterways are shallowest at the

The 'rule of the road': 'keep to the right' in straight sections.

edges. Keen eyes will notice where stones have tumbled from the bank, or the local youth have uncharitably dislodged a parapet. The propeller could be in danger here.

The deepest water is in the middle on straight sections, and towards the outside of curves. Very occasionally – though rarely inland – buoys or posts will be used to mark the channel in a river. Maritime convention is often followed: for craft coming in from the sea, red markers are left to port (to the 'left'), black markers to starboard (to the 'right'). Buoyage changes commencing in 1977 will eventually replace black markers with green ones in estuaries. Otherwise river channels usually lie two-thirds of the way across towards the outside of a bend.

On canals, the channel has often been carved by the passage of vessels, and it is a useful guideline to imagine the biggest possible craft that might use a waterway (that rare species, the dredger, perhaps) and to follow the line that she would have to take. She would be compelled to take all corners very wide, and in order to fit through the bridge she would get lined up well beforehand: the channel will probably do the same.

On a tight bend a heavy boat may have to take the corner wide, and small craft must either hold back or go over towards the inside.

The Rule of the Road

Most inland waterways have speed limits, but a reasonable speed is often lower than that prescribed. Injunctions to travel at 4 mph (the limit on many canals) or 6 to 8 mph (on rivers) can only provide a rough guide. There are times when 2 mph is much too fast:

1. When the vessel is sending a breaking wave against the bank. This causes hundreds of pounds worth of damage, incenses the authorities, puts up the licence fees and drenches anglers. Wash has effectively destroyed many good waterways. It can be seen *in extremis* on the Caledonian Canal in Scotland, where the culprits have been hardy fishermen speeding from one coast to the other. Please do not follow their appalling example.

2. When passing moored craft. The suction of a passing vessel can bang them together, pull out mooring spikes or empty someone's dinner.

3. When approaching a tight bend, a confined or congested area, or when meeting other craft. Vessels passing too quickly get drawn together. It is politer, and safer, to proceed slowly.

These rules are regularly broken, often by those who should know better. They will be more closely observed if waterway users follow an old custom, long forgotten on the roads; that is to greet one another with some reasonable show of concern. On the Continent, a simian arm is pushed forward in the wheelhouse, with the palm upright; on British rivers and canals, the time-honoured greeting is 'ardyerdo'.

The buoyage convention on rivers has black buoys to starboard of vessels heading upstream, red buoys to port. (Commencing in 1977, green will gradually replace black on starboard-hand marks.)

In meeting and passing other craft, the general rule is to pass 'port side to', or, in waterway parlance, to Keep to the Right. Possible exceptions are in a wide river, where it is sometimes the custom for craft going against the current to keep well to either side; or on tight bends, where large or unwieldy vessels may have no option but to stick to the outside. It is most unwise in this instance to 'stand on your rights', even if you have any, and a safer course is to keep out of the way.

If time allows it is good practice to wait before a tight bend if another boat is already coming round it. If a vessel wishes to take the 'wrong' side she should, strictly speaking, signal her intentions. On the Continent this is always done, either by displaying a blue flag on the side on which you are to pass, or by sound signals. In Britain the steerer may gesticulate wildly or do nothing at all. Sound signals are unfortunately rare. If in doubt: slow down, as always, and signal your own intentions:

1. A single blast on the horn or siren signifies that a vessel is turning to starboard (to her 'right') and will follow the normal Rule of the Road.

2. Two blasts signify turning to port (to her 'left') and an oncoming vessel will pass on the 'wrong' side.

3. Three blasts mean that a vessel's engines are going astern (though she may not yet be moving astern).

A single long blast on the horn is also the standard method of drawing attention, at swing bridges and blind corners or when, as occasionally on bigger waterways, red and green light signals control traffic at keeper-operated locks. It is advisable to make it a long blast, to avoid confusion with passing cars, or the single blast meaning a turn to starboard.

On rivers, rowers, scullers and, occasionally, swimmers will be encountered. They should be avoided; likewise sailing craft, which are best tackled by slowing right down in the centre of the stream. As a generalization, sailing and rowing boats have right of way. Their movements may appear haphazard, but generally they will be following a distinct pattern, often involving 'tacking' or zig-zagging into the wind. Once this has been defined it is usually possible to pass behind or 'astern' of a sailing

Power and sail on the Norfolk Broads. The sailing boat is obliged to 'tack' on a zig-zag course, in order to progress against the wind. The motor boat has waited, and will now pass astern of her.

boat. Rowing or sculling boats tend to be in mid-stream when going with the current, and at the edges when against it.

If in any doubt, at any time, slow right down. If deciding to alter course to avoid collision, do so in good time, and firmly. A sharp and determined alteration will convey your intention rapidly; a gradual or indecisive one may not.

Overtaking on a narrow waterway is a matter of courtesy. If the slower vessel is in sight of a lock, it is proper for the other to wait. In any event, it is sensible not to pass until waved by. This situation commonly arises on Continental canals, where laden barges are compelled to go slowly. The steerer of the barge may be obliged to stay in mid-channel, and will beckon another vessel past only if it is reasonable to do so.

At tunnels or narrow bridges it is again wise to go cautiously. On British canals craft are usually permitted to enter a tunnel at any time, provided there is room inside for two 7 ft boats to pass. When meeting another, it is safest to slow to a crawl and to scrape the boat along the right hand wall when passing. A blast on the horn when entering warns other craft in good time, and the headlight should be switched on throughout. It

Islington Tunnel on the Regent's Canal in London. Narrow craft may pass inside, but should slow right down when meeting. (Robert Shopland, *Waterways World*)

is particularly important to keep the light on when emerging, lest some other vessel should enter unawares.

With a wide-beamed headlamp, of the type most useful in tunnels, it is also possible to travel at night. Hire companies often forbid it, and in general it should only be undertaken, and with great caution, by the knowledgeable and responsible. On some waterways, night-time travel is expressly prohibited; on others the full navigational display may be required, with port, starboard, stern, and masthead light.

Choosing a mooring place

It used to be the custom to moor at least one full boat's length from the entrance to a lock. This allowed room for sudden arrivals and for craft working through in turn, such as a boat and butty. It is still wise to leave the area clear, for there will be the occasional craft borne on the wind, or too deep-drafted to reach the bank at any other point.

Likewise, it is sensible to moor clear of any bridge, while those who have steered an unwieldy vessel around a bend will know how vulnerable are those who moor on the outside of it. As a general principle, mooring on bends is best avoided, as is mooring near bridges, near locks, or between them when they are closely spaced – overnight leakage can leave you marooned.

If lying at a staging, thoughtful boat handlers moor close together to allow space for late arrivals. If mooring outside other vessels it is essential not to block the channel, and polite to ask permission. With commercial craft, 6 am starts and the presence of Alsatian dogs are equal hazards. It is a traditional courtesy not to lie close to a boatman's cabin, and to avoid peering inside. If walking across such a boat, please do so at the opposite end and as quietly and neatly as possible.

Ropes

Ropework is really the key to good boat handling on inland waterways. On light boats it is possible to get by with clothesline, the granny knot and india-rubber arms, but the sage use of rope makes everything safer and more relaxing. Before plunging into the nuances of coiling, and so on, it is simpler to consider a few knots.

Knots represent the mystique of ocean sailing, and there are books with diagrams of thousands. Most of these are useless, unless the vessel is carrying casks of tamara, or has clew garnets abaft the topsails. For canal use it is important to know about five knots, plus three more that are best avoided.

In choosing a knot for a particular job, it is helpful to visualize the time when it will have to be undone, perhaps in a hurry. Numbers 5 and 6 in the following list are particularly useful, since they can be released when a rope is bar-taut – an important point in locks. The others are self-explanatory. The first three are included in the hope that they can be avoided.

1. The reef knot – a neat but potentially lethal knot that tends to undo of its own accord, particularly when joining ropes

Not recommended – the reef knot.

of different size. It is used for tying reefs in mainsails, but on rivers or canals it is best forgotten.

2. The granny – the proverbial bad knot, since it is a reef with the ends the wrong way round. Given the choice it may be preferred, if only because it will not come undone. It merely jams inextricably.

Not recommended – the granny.

.3. The clove hitch. This is recommended in several handbooks, but is another with problems. Tied properly it is very effective – until you try to undo it. Its tendency to work loose when taking an on-and-off strain makes it unsuitable for dinghy painters or mooring lines.

Nor recommended – the clove hitch.

4. The round turn and two half hitches – a modification of the clove hitch, and a slightly better proposition for mooring posts, since the round turn takes up most of the pull, and the 'half hitches' are unlikely to be drawn too tight.

A round turn and two half-hitches.

5. The figure-of-eight – the obvious candidate for cleats or double bollards. Three or four complete 'eights' will normally

hold anything, although very slippery rope occasionally requires one or two more. It is generally a mistake to put a final tuck or hitch on the line, as this will nullify the object of the exercise. So too will winding the inner or 'standing' part of the rope back around itself: under load, it cannot be undone at all. If a mooring line falls slack it should always be undone completely in order to tighten it. Improvisations with the standing part invite disaster.

The figure-of-eight. The final tuck shown in the last two stages is not necessary, and may jam. Further figure-of-eights are preferable, with the end left free.

Not recommended – using the 'standing part', the portion that takes the tension, around a cleat. It may be impossible to undo.

6. The canalman's (or lighterman's) hitch. This has many names, but it is the classic inland waterway knot, since it can be released against tremendous pull, at any time. A close relative to the figure-of-eight, it can be applied to a single bollard or post. The first stage is to take a turn around the bollard, and then to tuck a loop beneath the standing part, as in the illustration. The loop is then dropped over the post, and the process can be repeated *ad infinitum*. It is not necessary to tie or tuck the end; it may just be left lying.

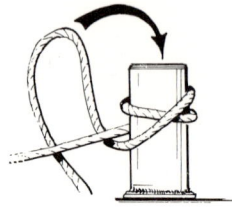

The 'canalman's hitch'. Further turns can be made, and the process repeated.

7. The bowline – the standard method of forming a noose, and a firm knot that still undoes very easily. In locks it provides a convenient loop for laying over a bollard, and the line can then be pulled in from on board. The bowline takes a little practice, and it is necessary when tying to check that the knot has been properly formed.

The bowline.

8. The sheet bend – a good method of joining two ropes together, whether of equal or unequal size. Once again, this is a knot that needs careful assembly, but is readily undone after use.

The sheet bend. Care is needed in drawing the lines tight. If the larger one is thick or stiff, take the smaller line around it twice, passing under itself as shown.

Taking a turn

The first stage in several of these knots is to wind the rope around a bollard or stump. The process is often used in stopping a boat, and a single turn of rope can absorb an enormous pull. It involves a little practice and rather more caution: it is vital to keep fingers clear at all times, and if the boat is moving it will be necessary to slip the rope (let it slide round the bollard) to stop it jerking. The alternatives could be a snapped rope or, more likely, the removal of a bollard from the ground or deck. The skill lies in getting the rope around the post in good time, in drawing it tight and in letting it slip again before bringing the boat to a halt. A double turn will hardly slip at all, and may jam solid on itself, so it is to be avoided if possible.

Taking a turn. Some handlers make a point of winding the rope in the same direction, usually clockwise, as when coiling; but this is less important than letting the rope slip a little in order to take the strain, and keeping one's fingers well clear of the bollard.

Mooring

There are many methods of mooring. The simplest is to drop two nooses (from your bow and stern) over some convenient bollards. In practice, flying leaps and the penetration of hawthorn bushes are common. Where traffic is light, mooring stakes may be used. They should be neither too close to the towpath edge, nor in the line of passers-by. If there are rings, the rope may be doubled back through the ring to the boat, or a piece of wood thrust through a loop and then drawn tight; but usually the knot to use is a round turn and two half hitches.

If moored where wash is a problem, a 'spring' can be useful – an extra line running from the shore back or forward to a contrary tying point on board. This will restrain the boat from surging.

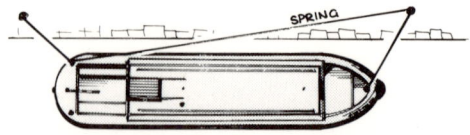

Mooring with a spring, to prevent surging.

If mooring to a post that is already in use by another boat it is helpful to pass the noose of your rope upwards through any other loop before dropping it over the top of the post. This enables either craft to cast off without disturbing the other's line.

42

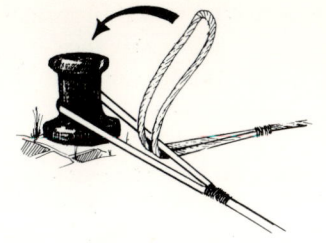

Passing one noose through another allows either craft to leave without disturbing the other's line.

Coiling and throwing

Throwing a rope is one of those classic boating situations from which the bystanders extract most of the fun. Frequent mistakes are throwing in a hurry, and throwing from too far away.

As far as possible, the ropes on a boat ought to be kept carefully coiled. It is best to avoid coiling around the arm and elbow, or laying down the rope in tiddly flat spirals (known as 'cheesing'). In either case the rope will tangle when used. The standard manner with ordinary rope is to coil it down on deck in as tidy a heap as possible. It is essential to work *away* from an end that has been tied, in order to shake out any kinks. It is also important, though not quite as vital, to work in a clockwise direction, and if the crew can be persuaded, to wind it around bollards or stumps in the same clockwise manner. The rope will be less likely to snarl up or kink as a result.

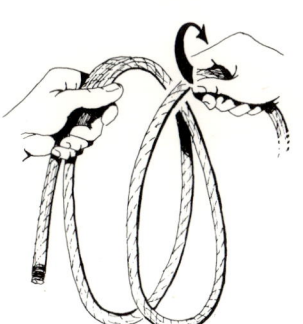

With conventional rope, coiling is usually done clockwise.

Experienced rope handlers usually sort through a rope first, passing the entire length through their hands to get kinks and knots out, and coiling only at the second attempt.

If throwing is called for, the coiling can often be done in the hands, again working away from a fixed end, and towards the free end of the line. The swing of the arms will measure out the size of each loop: over-large loops tangle and are harder to throw. Then, holding the rope in the hands, the coil is carefully divided into two. Half goes into one hand for throwing, the rest stays in the other ready to pay out over the open fingers. No matter what the crisis, it always pays to do this preparation carefully. If the rope is massive, some will have to be left on the deck; but that in the hands is still evenly divided, half and half.

The actual throwing is done underhand, throwing that half of the rope. The rest of the coil should follow. If it does not, and the rope falls short, there is no alternative but to pull it all back in, and to systematically start at the beginning. It is a common feature of these operations that those who are not doing the throwing will gallop about with imploring looks or otherwise persuade the handler to throw too early. Ignore them: the cool approach always pays dividends.

Two other tips: do not throw more than you can manage; and if on a large vessel with heavy ropes, keep a light line handy for sending over first. A heavier rope can be knotted onto this, once contact has been established.

Throwing the coil, by dividing it in two and then throwing half. Do not let go of the other end, as shown, unless the line is very long, or already fixed!

Locks

To the astonishment of Continental authorities, many locks in Britain are completely unsupervised, and boat crews are left to their own devices. Locks are thus rather daunting, or at first bemusing; but they are equally looked upon as stimulating, and the instruments of healthy exercise. In the simplest cases, locks can be worked in just over three minutes apiece, and aggressive crews tend to devour them, like pigeons in pursuit of bread. At the other end of the scale are locks that are worked by keepers, such as those on the upper Thames, where the atmosphere can be mellow, and time of little account.

Equipment and terminology

No two locks are alike, but all work on the same principle. A boat is enclosed in a chamber with gates at either end. Water is then let in or out, as the occasion demands, to float the boat to a higher or lower level. The gates at one end may then be opened, and the boat sails away.

Like so many things, locks have their own terminology. The *gates* are obvious enough, but the sluices that admit the water are frequently known as *paddles*. The paddle is a sliding panel that is usually hidden from view, either in the bowels of the earth, where it operates in a culvert, or sometimes at the bottom of the gate itself. The operating mechanism is located above it, usually as a cluster of worn cogwheels.

If a paddle is *in* a gate, it is known as a *gate paddle*. The others are *ground paddles*. The upstream end of a lock is generally referred to as the *top*, the other end as the *bottom* (sometimes the *tail*). All the paddles at the upstream end may thus be referred to as *top paddles*, those at the downstream end as *bottom*

Letting in the water on the Upper Thames. Here the 'paddles' are known as 'sluices' once again, and in this instance are wound open with a handwheel.

paddles. The distinction can be useful in the hysteria of incorrect operation.

The paddles are generally worked by means of a steel key or *windlass*, which boat crews carry themselves. The windlass is an L-shaped handle with a square socket at one end to fit the mechanism. Naturally there is more than one size, but two windlasses will operate most of the do-it-yourself locks in Britain, and windlasses are often provided with two sockets on one handle.

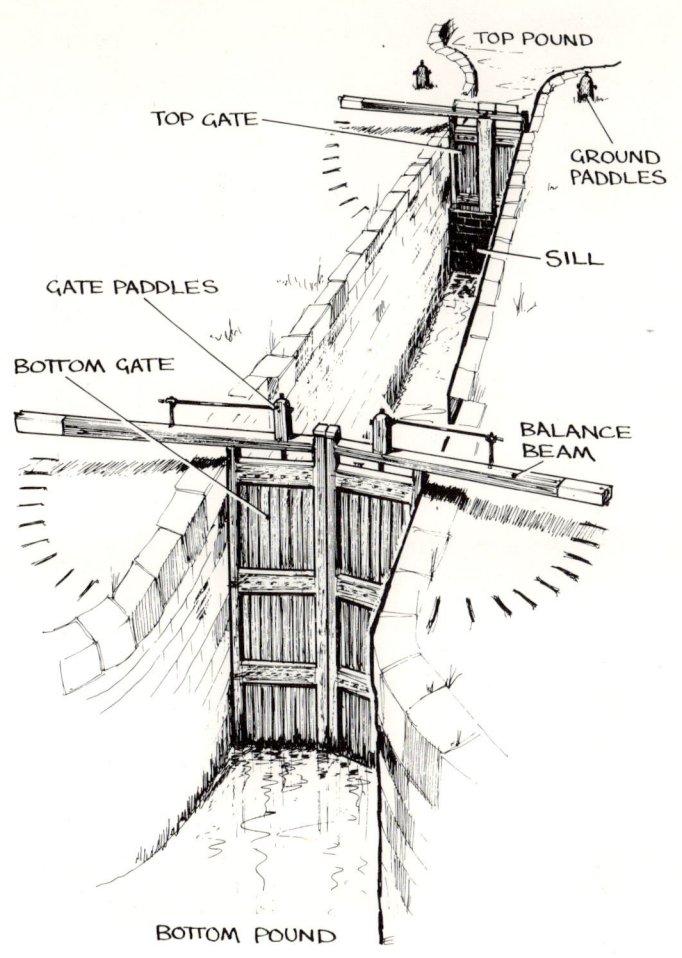

The terminology of the lock.

The mechanisms vary considerably, but almost every one
will have a *pawl* or a ratchet of some kind, an iron catch to
prevent the paddle from dropping down after winding. In its
commonest form the paddle is opened by winding upwards a
toothed bar, and closed again by lowering it. A tidemark of
congealed grease will show the point to which a paddle should
drop (descend) in order to be properly closed. The process of
opening is often referred to as *drawing* the paddles.

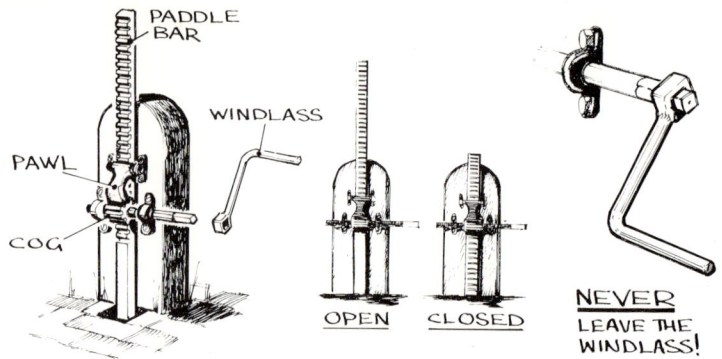

Basic paddle mechanisms. It is dangerous to leave or let go of a windlass on a wound-up paddle.

Other useful terms are the word *pound*, which refers to the stretch of canal between two locks, and the *sill*, sometimes spelled *cill*. The sill is a ledge of unrelenting stone that projects into the lock from beneath the top gates. It is important not to catch the boat on it when descending, by lying too close to the gates.

The gates themselves are often opened by means of projecting *balance beams*, against which it is customary to lean with a stoical expression, pushing backwards with the shoulders. No lock gate can be opened until the water levels on either side are exactly equal. Once this is achieved the gates should swing easily.

48

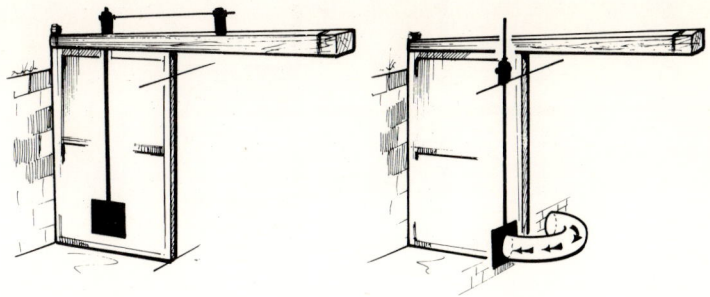

Left:
A gate paddle, simply a shutter over an opening in the lock gate.
Right:
A ground paddle, in which an underground culvert lets water in or out of a lock.

Working a lock

A good example is provided by a typical narrow lock of the English canals. This will almost certainly be worked by boat crews themselves.

Before a boat can enter, it is essential that the water inside the lock is at the same level as in the pound in which the boat is floating:

To fill the lock, make sure that the bottom gates and paddles are firmly closed, then open the top paddles.

To empty the lock, make sure that the top gates and paddles are firmly closed, then open the bottom paddles.

Once the lock is ready, the boat may be taken inside either with ropes or, more conveniently, under her own power. A vessel of 'narrow boat' proportions should just fit comfortably. If it is possible to manage without fend-offs it is sensible to do so, since they catch on gates and jam against the walls. Tough canal boats may also pass through without ropes, although some understanding of the motion inside the lock is necessary, and it is safer for someone to stay at the controls. Don't attempt this without experience.

Frailer vessels will have to be fendered and tied. It is common in England to lead lines ashore and to hang onto them from there, but with larger craft a safe practice is to drop a noose over a bollard on shore and to adjust the length from on board.

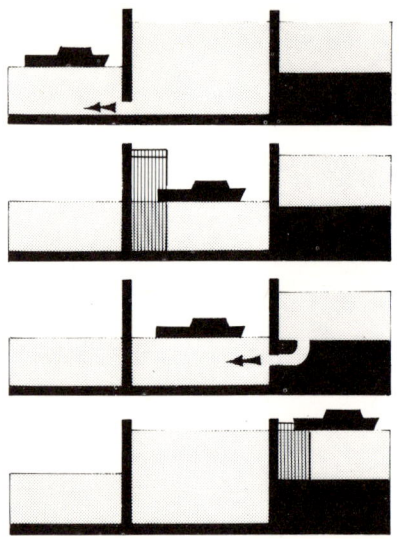

Going up

1. With top gates and paddles closed, the paddles are 'drawn' at the other end to prepare the lock.
2. Once the levels are equal, the bottom gates may be opened and the boat can enter.
3. With bottom gates and paddles closed again, the top paddles can be 'drawn' to fill the lock.
4. Once the levels are equal, the gates may be opened for the vessel to leave.

It is important that lines cannot jam. The figure-of-eight around the deck bollard is particularly useful for this purpose.

If the boat is ascending, the bottom gates and paddles should be checked after she has entered, to see that they are properly closed. The paddles at the top can then be 'drawn', winding carefully, with the pawl always in position against the gear. Sometimes paddles are drawn too rapidly; ground paddles are usually the gentler, and these should be operated first if possible. Once the levels are equal, the gates can be opened and the boat may leave. Officially, you must close all gates and paddles again afterwards and it is often wise to do so.

Descending in a lock is a much smoother process, provided

Going down

1. The chamber is prepared. With bottom gates and paddles all closed, water is admitted by raising or 'drawing' a top paddle.
2. When levels are equal, the gates may be opened and the boat can enter.
3. The top gates are closed again and the top paddles 'dropped'. Opening the paddles at the other end will then drain out the water.
4. When the lock has emptied, the gates can be opened for the boat to leave.

that ropes, if any, are tended, and the vessel is kept well clear of the sill. After bringing the boat into the chamber and closing the top gates and paddles, those at the bottom end may be drawn, until the gates are open and the vessel is ready to leave.

In broad locks the system is exactly the same, and the only basic difference is that there is more room to swing about. If the chamber is shared with other craft, careful ropework and fending off may be necessary. If there is a lock-keeper he may take the lines, but he does so to ensure smooth working and as a gesture of courtesy. It remains the crew's responsibility to tend their own ropes.

When leaving a broad lock with a narrow beamed boat, it is not always necessary to open both gates.

51

Some 'do's' and don'ts'

Inevitably, there are several of these:

1. In winding a paddle, always check that the pawl is engaged first. Some are worn; others bounce free during winding. If this happens the pawl should be immediately re-engaged, keeping a vice-like grip upon the windlass at the same time. Likewise, when winding down a paddle, the windlass must be firmly grasped throughout. A paddle will often close under gravity, but it can be damaged in the process. It is better to wind it down, checking that it travels all the way.

2. It is most dangerous to leave a windlass attached to a wound up or 'drawn' paddle. Should the mechanism slip, the windlass can fly free and deliver a brutal injury; it should be kept in the hands at all times, until put back on board.

3. Crossing a lock demands an obvious circumspection. Some of the worst locks are on the Grand Canal in Ireland, where the footboards are loosely hung on chains. The old sailing rule is best: keep a hand free for hanging on, if needs be.

4. While waiting for a lock to be prepared, the boat is best kept clear of it. When the lock is filling, water will be drawn towards it. When emptying, there are some unexpected eddies. Surprisingly, boats waiting below a lock are often drawn forwards also, and it is possible to harpoon the gates with vigour.

5. If ascending without ropes, the safest place in a narrow lock is near the bottom gates, or right at the other end, with the bow actually rubbing the top sill or the gates above it. The backwash will hold the boat in this position, but care must be taken not to draw the paddles too swiftly and wash the foredeck. In broad locks there can be other odd effects: drawing a ground paddle will often bring the boat over towards that side, whereas opening a gate paddle will wash her across the chamber.

6. Whether ascending or descending, watch the boat at all times, and be prepared to drop all paddles in a crisis (such as getting stuck on or under some part of the lock, ropes jamming so they can't slide or be released, or someone falling in).

Saving water

Water is an immensely valuable commodity on a canal, and many have closed for the lack of it. Storage is in reservoirs, and

Saving water. Three boats share a narrow lock.
(Robert Shopland, *Waterways World*)

there are laborious systems of pumping and feeder channels that
pass unnoticed by the casual visitor.

Obviously it is imprudent to leave paddles open at either end
of a lock, but there are also subtler means by which water can
be saved:

1. Sharing locks. Even narrow locks can sometimes be shared, and with careful operation it is possible for two, conceivably three, craft to work through together. If ascending, the toughest boat should go first and lie with her stem resting against the sill or top gates. In broad locks it is safer for narrow boats to lie side by side, again as far forward as possible, with any frailer craft behind. Naturally some care must be taken, and a pillar of sobriety should operate the paddles.

2. Working turns. If a lock contains boats every time it is operated, then it is being efficiently used. So, if another vessel is in sight and the lock is prepared, it is sensible to let her work through first. The chamber is then ready for the boat proceeding in the opposite direction, and so on. The practice, known as 'working turns', is sometimes insisted on during dry weather.

3. Lock-wheeling is the canal term for sending someone ahead to prepare the locks. If undertaken on a bicycle, as the name suggests, it can be an adventure in itself. If speed is the aim, it will help a boat considerably. In the later days of commercial traffic, the English towpaths were thick with whirling figures (and cursing anglers). It is possible to be too enthusiastic, however, and to work so far ahead that boats coming the other way are deprived of their own opportunities. Shrewd lock-wheeling can benefit everyone, by the organized working of locks, but it is wise to work within sight or earshot of your own boat.

4. Closing all gates and paddles after leaving. This is often an official requirement, and it stems from two considerations: sloppy lock operation, and the fact that many locks leak. In practice an enclosed lock can be a dangerous thing for passers-by to fall into, while it is maddening for those on another boat to have the gates closed in their faces. A little judgement is called for. If traffic is heavy, gates may perhaps be left. But in the evening, or on little used waterways, or if there are any signs of leaking, it is public-spirited to close everything. In periods of drought, this policy is likely to be insisted on.

Some exceptional locks

The locks already discussed are of the commonest type, but there are several departures from the norm. Listed below are some of the more distinctive variations.

54

Guillotines

On the River Nene and other Fenland waterways, many locks have vertically lifting or 'guillotine' gates. The lower gate rises within a steel frame. The upper gates, known in this area as *pointing doors*, operate in the conventional manner. A basic distinction with guillotine locks is that the sliding gate operates as a sluice or paddle as well. By winding it upwards, water is released, and by winding it further boats may enter or leave underneath.

Two cautions:

1. Raise the guillotine a fraction only to allow water to leave. Raising it quickly causes violent surging in the lock.

2. Each lock must be left with the pointing doors (upper gates) open and the guillotine closed. You thus have the doubtful pleasure of working each one of these extremely heavy locks twice.

Guillotine gates are usually stiff. Their purpose is often flood

A guillotine lock on the River Nene. Someone must stay behind to lower the gate again and refill the chamber, unless another boat is coming the other way.

control, and this is not an advantage from the boatman's point of view. In flood conditions the guillotine may have been raised a little to drain away water. All gates will then be padlocked with the pointing doors left open, and having recovered from a precipitate arrival on the flood current, you will not be permitted to work the lock anyway.

In normal use, a key must be obtained from the canal authorities to release the winding gear. Ordinary windlasses may then be employed. The usual care must be taken, and particular care when the gate is *curved*, as the mechanism is complicated, and a build-up of energy may cause the windlass to spin.

Guillotine locks are common on the Continent, where they also rise up from the canal bed. Being electrically operated by resident keepers, they pose few problems.

Staircases

In staircase locks the bottom gates of one chamber act as the top gates of the next. There are no intervening pounds. Staircases are wasteful of water and they can hold up traffic, since it is not usually possible for boats to pass in them. They were built only when circumstances demanded, but there are several on British canals. Most notable are the eight chambers at Banavie on the Caledonian Canal, the 'Five-rise' at Bingley on the Leeds & Liverpool, and two flights of five at Foxton in Leicestershire.

In theory a staircase may be worked by emptying one chamber into the one below; but if the one below is already full, the water spills across the towpath. The one below must therefore be emptied first, and so on.... Because of this, and to save water, *side ponds* are sometimes provided. These are small reservoirs to the side and the water is emptied into them through *side paddles*. Equally, the water can be drained back into the chambers if desired. Arrangements differ, and a very systematic approach is called for when working.

The usual pitfalls are draining a lock into one that is already full, leaving the wrong paddles open, or dumping a boat on the masonry at the bottom of a chamber, since it is possible to drain off a lock completely. It may be a consolation to those readers who are kicking and screaming at the prospect, that local help is generally available.

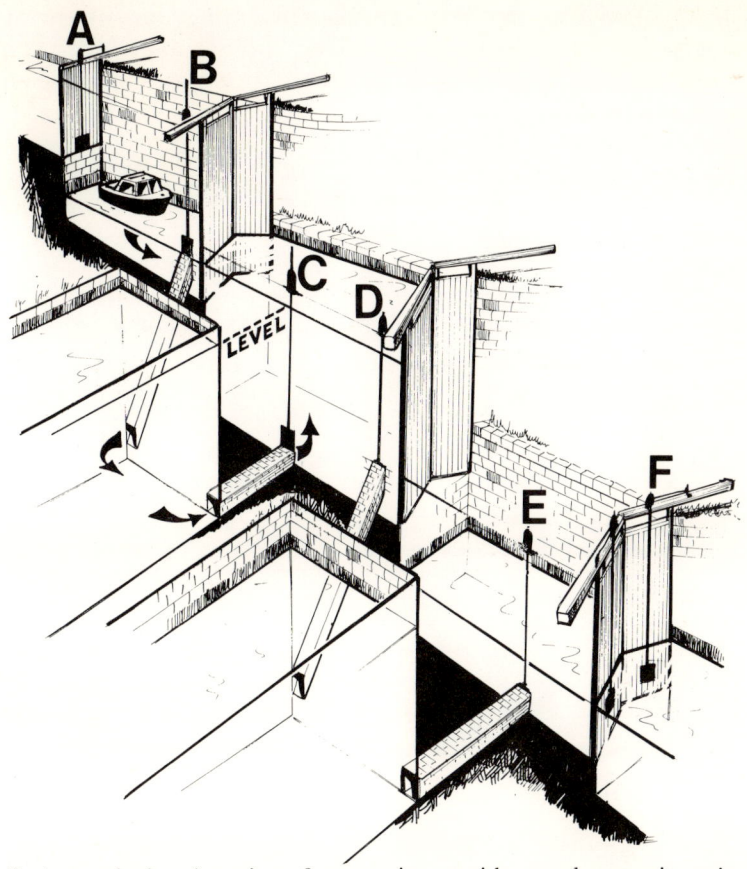

Staircase locks. A series of reservoirs or side ponds permit staircase locks to be emptied or filled without directly taking water from one another. Paddle A enables the top chamber to be filled from the canal above. If this is closed and B is opened the lock will drain into the reservoir alongside. Opening C will fill the next chamber, while D can empty it. E and F permit filling and emptying the bottom chamber.

Side ponds

These little reservoirs used to be a common feature at ordinary locks, but out of parsimony they have been neglected. If they work at all, and have not totally silted up, they can be a useful means of saving water. A full lock can be drained into an empty side pond, until the levels equalize. The side paddle is then closed and the rest of the lock emptied in the normal way. When next filling the lock, some of the water from the side pond is let in first, and so on.

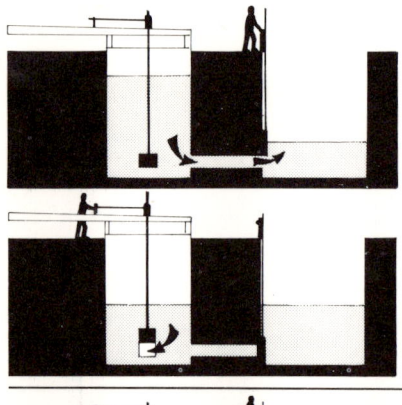

A side paddle enables the lock to be partially emptied into a small reservoir alongside – the side pond.

Once the levels have equalized the side paddle is closed and the rest of the lock emptied in the normal way.

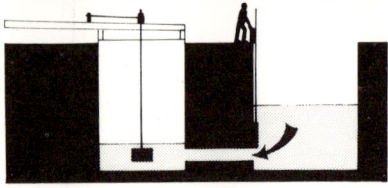

When next filling, water can be saved by taking some from the side pond instead.

Some oddities

Occasionally two locks are to be found side by side. The one most convenient should be used. If the equipment is in working order, a paddle between the two may enable the other chamber to be used as a side pond.

On the Leeds & Liverpool Canal in particular, there are many varieties of paddle, known regionally as 'cloughs'. Those operated by a simple wooden arm should always be closed to permit the gate to open fully, otherwise a wide boat, or two smaller craft working side by side, may jam in the entrance. On this waterway, as on several others, special keys are needed to unlock the gear at locks and swing bridges and these are generally obtained at either end of the waterway. Once released, much of the equipment has fixed windlasses or operating levers.

Some paddles are enclosed in casings, making it difficult to see at a distance whether they are closed or drawn. Examples are those on the Grand Union Canal north of Braunston, which have tiny inspection holes, and a new hydraulic type, introduced at random, which has a minute pointer. Hydraulic paddles are slow when winding down for closure – a disadvantage in an emergency.

On the Calder & Hebble Canal a large handspike or lever is used for raising paddles and fits into sockets on a small operating wheel. On the Thames, when the keepers are off duty, it is possible to manually operate many of the electrified locks by spinning a handwheel. There are many other minor variations on the basic principles of lock working.

The Things That Happen

Minor collisions and bumping the bank

Collision damage can be minimized by putting the engine astern, or by deft use of fenders. Whatever the crisis, it pays to let the engine idle for a moment, and then to increase speed gradually. Revving up too quickly when going astern will cause the propeller to 'cavitate' or draw in air, and render it ineffective.

At all costs avoid interposing any part of the human frame between boat, bank, or lock gate. It is tempting to stick out feet sometimes, but the momentum of small craft is considerable, and no boat is worth the sacrifice. Dropping a fender over the side is another matter, and the shrewd may care to keep a fat one handy. At no time is it sensible to use a boathook for staving off disaster. The sight of an inland mariner standing on the bow like Captain Ahab, harpoon in hand, can make the stoutest hearts quail. The result will be damage to the ribs or to some other vessel. Boathooks are best kept for retrieving objects from the surface, for poling when aground, or, very occasionally, for gentle prods against the bank when moving off.

It is always dangerous to fend off with arms or legs.

Bridges and trees

Low bridges are frequent on canals, and coupled with passengers' habits of lying on the roof or balancing on the side decks,
they are a definite hazard. It is up to the steerer to be cautious,
and to have no fear of warning the crew loudly and in good
time. If the boat is turning, the stern can swing sideways quite
rapidly and bring the cabin roof or sides against an overhang.

Swing and lift bridges are also common, and they are usually
worked by boat crews themselves. The same sense of caution
is necessary, and on lift bridges in particular it is vital that no-
one should risk being trapped against the forward end of the
cabin.

Avoid overhanging trees: they too inflict damage, and often
contain fish-hooks. A springy branch can easily pluck gear off
the cabin top.

A lift bridge on the southern portion of the Oxford Canal. Crew
should keep well clear as the boat passes through.

61

Going aground

Though frequent on shallow waterways, this is not generally serious. With experience it is possible to sense when a boat is running out of the channel and to slow her down. Oddly enough, steering back towards the centre does not always help, as the stern must first of all swing away and will often end up on the mud as well. Much depends on hull form. With vessels of the 'narrow boat' type it often pays to steer further *into* the shallows. This keeps the stern clear of them, so that it may be swung to and fro later, either with the engine, the long shaft, or in extreme cases by using ropes.

As a general principle it pays to get any part of the boat mov-

Boat handling situations. The craft above the lock are sensibly moored well clear of it, but those towards the outside of the bend may be vulnerable to large craft sweeping wide. Below the lock, boats have moored close in order to leave room for later arrivals. The vessel coming downstream will turn to face the current before coming alongside.

ing during a grounding, either backwards, forwards, or sideways. The direction is often immaterial, for the general levering action will usually free the portion that is stuck. In serious cases it is sometimes possible to interpose planks between boat and bank and utilize the momentum generated by swinging. Going astern sometimes helps a little, through the action of the propeller pushing water underneath the hull.

Fouled propellers

Polythene is the biggest enemy and on the worst canals it is also possible to get wire, sacks and the steel binding from packing cases. By comparison weed is easily dealt with.

The symptoms of a fouled propeller are juddering, vibration and an uneven wash. Many canal boats now have an access hatch in the bottom over the prop, which makes things easy, but it is important to *stop* the motor first (putting it in neutral is insufficient as a precaution) and to check that the hatch is actually well above the water level. If it isn't the boat will start to sink, and in the panic engendered it is easy to put the hatch back on the wrong way round.

Other measures are putting the engine into neutral, then briefly into reverse; (or, with it *stopped*, prodding with a boathook, dangling upside down with a breadknife, or getting into the water yourself.

SOME LESS COMMON SITUATIONS

Lack of water

There can be several causes of this: drought, inept paddle winding, or leaking lock gates. A useful preliminary is to walk the length of any shallow section and investigate the cause. On narrow canals, the occasional short pound may be found to be low. A boat can sometimes be washed along it, by allowing a *limited* amount of water through the lock up above. This will arrive in the form of a small wave, which will often rebound from the lock below and come sweeping back. Each time it passes, the boat will lift a little, and perhaps make progress.

It need hardly be added that the process should be handled responsibly and that the minimum of water be wasted. If in any doubt, seek out a canal officer, if one can be found, and obtain his assistance.

Towing

Although often prohibited by hire companies, towing other boats can be useful to the less constrained. If a waterway is wide enough, the most satisfactory method is to tie one craft alongside the other, with plenty of fend-offs in between. In addition to fore and aft ropes, a longer 'spring' will be necessary – a rope extending from the bow of the 'tug' to the stern of the other – and this will take most of the load. Strong attachment points and ropes that can be freed quickly are a necessity.

If towing on a long line, it is vital that it can be cast off in emergency, preferably from either end, but certainly from the boat being towed. The figure-of-eight or canalman's hitch (mentioned above) suggest themselves. Pitfalls are towing too quickly, or craft taking a sideways sheer. The towline should be attached centrally on the tug and well forward on the towed boat. If necessary a bridle of some kind will have to be arranged, to take the strain to really strong points and yet allow the towline to lead clear.

In very sheltered waters, it is sometimes possible for a light boat to be drawn up close behind the tug. Problems here are control, and fendering, but in a cross-wind on a narrow canal, this may be the only option.

Mooring on a bend. A narrow boat coming down on the current of the Lower Avon is compelled to take the corner wide in order to stay in the channel. The cruiser is vulnerable. For the record, the stern of the narrow boat, sweeping round in an arc, missed the moored boat by inches.

Bow hauling

This is the old waterway term for manual towing, 'bow' for some extraordinary reason being pronounced as in Bow Bells. Pulling a boat from the bank requires surprisingly little effort (and therein lies its efficiency as a means of propulsion). The secret is not to pull too hard, but to lean gently on the rope and let the boat travel at her own pace.

Bow hauling can be useful after a breakdown, and it is best accomplished by forming a bridle, as in the diagram. If the line were attached to the bow, the boat would be pulled towards the bank, if at the stern it would be turned away from it. A bridle combines both, and with experimentation it is possible to pull the boat quite easily with no-one steering her at all. If she turns towards you lengthen the rope a little; if she turns away, then pull it in. Provided the wind is not strong, a boat can be steered quite accurately by this method.

Bow hauling, with one person both pulling and controlling the boat.

Floods

Rivers can flood, even in summer. The increased current and low headroom under bridges will make upstream voyaging hard work, and a downstream passage heart-stopping. Local advice is a variable commodity, but that of lock-keepers is generally sound; please accept it.

If taking a chance, remember that the slackest water is right against the bank, and that you will always control the boat much better by first turning into the current. Turn *away* from any hazard, and if in doubt as to course, following the towpath will usually distinguish the navigation from a weir stream.

Ice

It is astonishing how even thin ice can stop a boat in her tracks. It can be broken, sometimes, by rocking the boat and so on, but the process is rarely worthwhile. Ice will cut deeply into wooden hulls, and, to a lesser extent, fibreglass. Only iron or steel boats will survive unscathed. It is a fallacy, however, that ice can crush a boat at her moorings. Ice pushed across by other vessels may sometimes do this, but the dangers chiefly lie in cracked pipes or skin fittings. Do not forget to close these when leaving the boat, and in winter drain the engine block and cooling system of all water.

Ice, a particular threat to wooden and fibreglass craft.

SOME UNCOMMON SITUATIONS

Tight locks and bridges

Some old canal boats are slightly over-sized, while the occasional lock may have distorted. Other hazards are debris behind the gates and the jolly habits of roadwork contractors, who build outwards at bridges, sink piles in the waterway, and drop heavy concrete blocks. The average boat will be unaffected, but that is no consolation to the others.

If wedged anywhere, the first stage is to locate the blockage and, if possible, to clear it. Bricks behind gates can with patience be removed with a boathook or long shaft. The traditional long-pronged rake or 'keb' is even better. Otherwise the going aground routine is best: to get the boat moving somehow, backwards, forwards, sideways, or up and down. The brief raising of paddles will lift a boat a little, so will putting the engine astern. Bitter experience will show that it is better to withdraw the boat than to push on through. Once she is out of the way, the obstacle can more reasonably be cleared.

Tight tunnels

There are not many of these, and at the tight ones a clearance gauge is often placed at either end. In times past, however, over-sized boats have stuck in several tunnels. The technique is to flood the boat's bilges a little, by undoing a water inlet cock perhaps; and it may be necessary to tilt the boat first by moving furnishings, so that water can move to the right end. The effect is similar to letting down the tyres of the apocryphal furniture van beneath a road bridge (and happens about as frequently).

Holes and sinking

Running onto a stake or an unusual stone can occasionally hole a boat, but she need not sink. Stage One is to locate the hole, Stage Two to deal with it. Only if either proves impossible should a crew consider abandoning, and if they take their time they can usually take off their valuables first. Few boats sink within seconds: there should be time to head for the shallows, if the boat is not actually impaled and immobile.

Leaks can be stopped by wedging them with rag, or, if available, clay. A potato might be useful, or even a dollop of grease. The best method is usually to construct a wooden pad and to wedge this down firmly with wooden blocks, perhaps using a cloth as a seal. Though their owners don't like it known, some boats have been going round in this condition for years.

Fire

A small fire is a big one getting started. Action must be swift. Tackle it immediately with extinguishers, or any other available means of smothering it. Try to cut down the air supply; prevent it reaching inflammables. Do not cut yourself off from help – on the Thames, for example, lock-keepers are trained in firefighting, but they need to reach the boat first.

Prevention is better than cure. Precautions are the sensible use of gas, with bottles in vented outdoor containers, carrying large extinguishers, fitting fireproof fuel lines, and the greatest care with petrol and naked flames. Inflammable gases can lie in the bottom of a boat for days, and the wise owner will first check by sniffing at floor level and under the floorboards before switching on the engine.

Well ablaze – a small cruiser on the Upper Thames.

Man overboard

This is always serious, even in a shallow canal. Make sure the engine is in neutral, and preferably switched off, if anyone is near the propeller. In locks, drop all paddles. Do not be frightened to make a fuss, even if the person can swim, or others think it funny; concussion, fright or broken limbs can make it more serious than they think.

In wide rivers, nautical practice should be followed. Keep at least one life ring handy, don't clutter it with lines or string that might snag, and throw it to the victim before doing anything else. Get someone to watch his position constantly, and in turning to pick the person up, remember the propeller again.

The 'Kiss of Life'

This simplified form of artificial respiration has saved many:

Lie victim on his/her back, press head backwards and lower jaw upwards.

Hold the nostrils closed and breathe air into the mouth, removing your own mouth each time. Repeat every 5 seconds (with children 3 seconds). With babies or very small children, don't force too much air in.

Clear victim's mouth of water, etc. by turning the head to one side.

Wider Waters –
Towards the Estuary

Sooner or later a river will meet the sea; and its last few miles will be less hospitable than the chuckling upper reaches, or the intimate little canals that join them.

Not quite 'inland', not yet the ocean, such territory tends to be overlooked in the guidebooks. There are several uncertain stretches in England: the passage through London, the links with the Wash, and the lower reaches of the Trent and York-shire Ouse. Such 'in-between' waterways may often be tackled by inland craft, with the right precautions:

1. Verification with the insurance company or hire operator of suitable cover or permission.

2. Getting hold of maps or charts. Stanford's Chart No. 6 of *The Lower Thames – Richmond to the Nore* covers the passage through London. The *Yorkshire Ouse from Trent Falls to York* and *Tidal Waters of the River Trent* are two exceptional regional guides, produced by Vincent Sissons of Guardian Offices, Worksop, Notts. Elsewhere local enquiry may have to be made.

3. Proper preparation of the boat. Familiarity with engine and fuel system is essential; personal buoyancy aids and at least one lifebuoy ready for throwing are considered vital by many; also the firm stowage of all movables, from pots of jam to the gas bottle, since small boats in particular can rock in the slightest chop, and it only takes one swing to transform a neat interior into chaos. Perhaps most important of all is good ground tackle – a decent anchor and chain – of which more anon.

4. Understanding the weather and tide. Rain does not mat-ter, save in flood: it is the wind that does most of the damage. While standard forecasts mention it occasionally, the Shipping

70

A typical tidal river, the Yorkshire Ouse, with a cruiser suitable for both estuary and sea use travelling downstream on the ebb.

Forecasts broadcast by the BBC four times a day give a better guide. Wind strengths are given on the Beaufort Scale, up to and occasionally beyond Force 8 for Full Gale. Such strengths, often terrifying at sea, can add a dimension of extreme unpleasantness even to sheltered water. Force 5 can be quite sufficient, particularly if the wind is blowing against a tidal stream. The Shipping Forecasts are given for set Sea Areas, of which Humber and Thames are two, and a little extrapolation will be necessary. If in doubt, it often pays to hear a succession of forecasts in order to build up an impression of the weather pattern, and in particular the rate of change.

The influence of the tide can come as a surprise, for not only does the level go up and down, with obvious consequences, but the stream flows in and out. The London River on a strong 'ebb' will generate a startling speed, the lower Trent, Ouse, and tidal Nene no less so.

The tide flows on roughly a twelve-and-a-half-hour cycle, but the distribution of 'ebb' and 'flood' are by no means equal. On the lower Trent, for example, the river floods (inwards from the sea) for less than three hours at many points, and ebbs (towards the sea) for the remaining nine-and-a-half. The diagrams on these pages indicate the timings of these currents on both the Trent and the Yorkshire Ouse, and since the flow can be as speedy as many boats might travel, it is useful to take advan-

The Trent's tidal pattern — Spring Tides

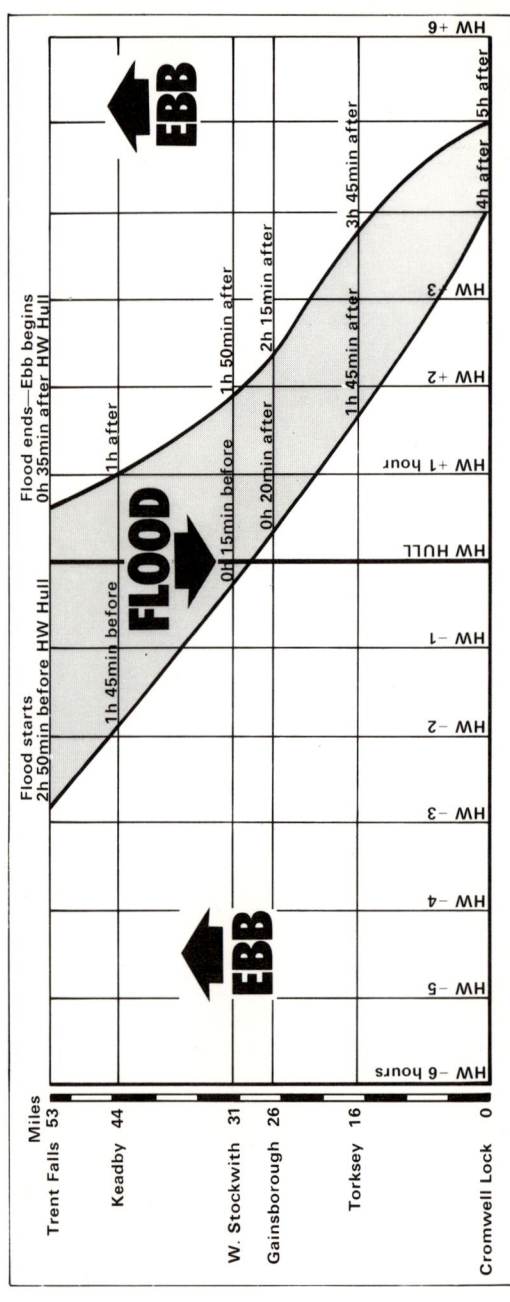

. . . and at Neap Tides

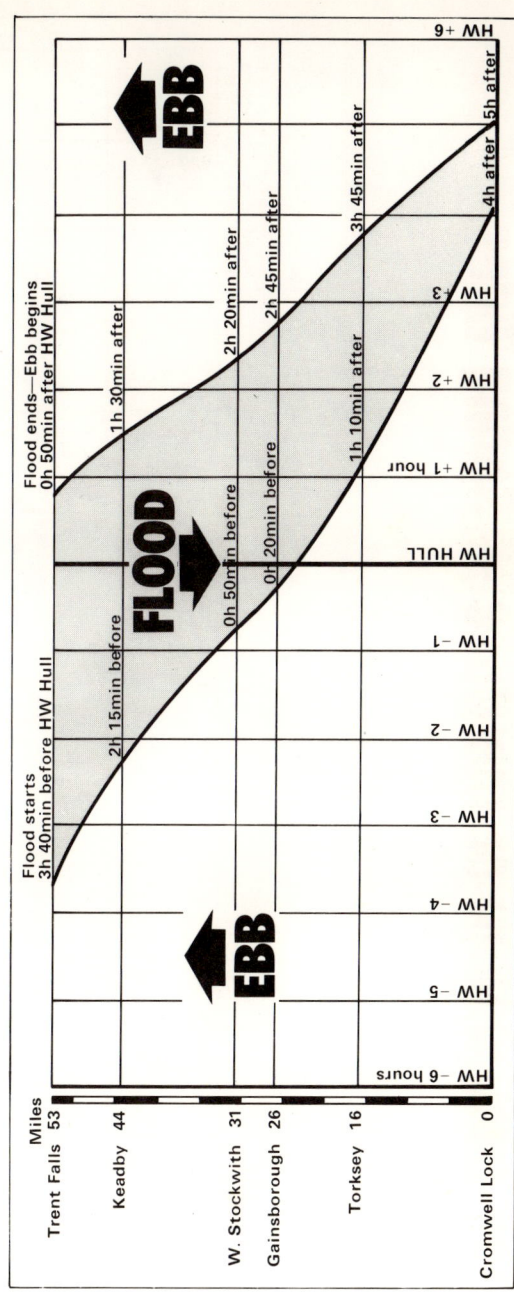

The tidal pattern of the Ouse — Spring Tides

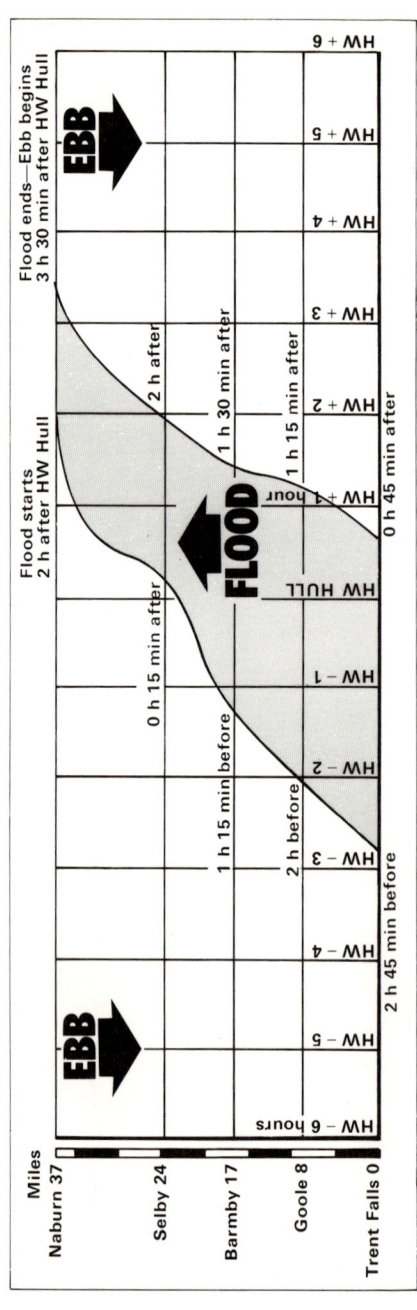

... and at Neap Tides

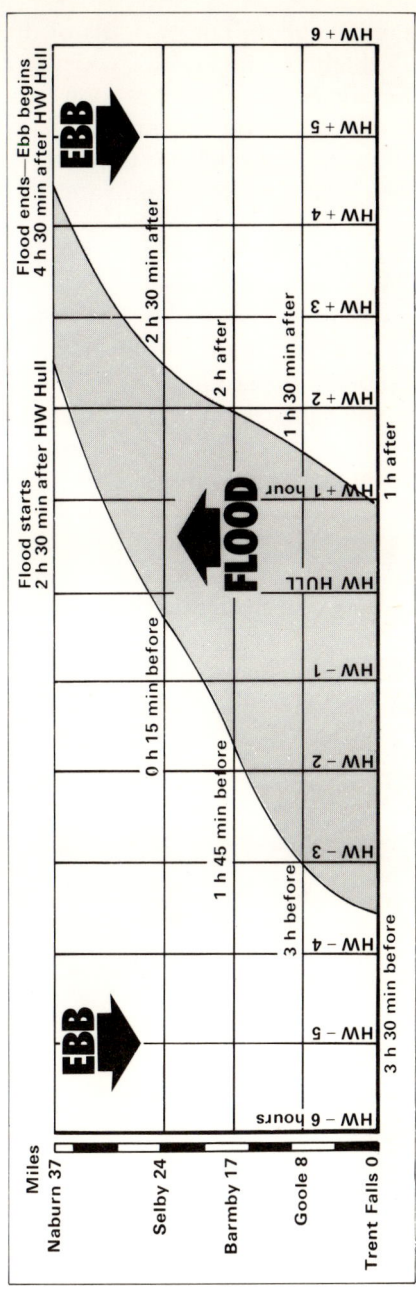

tage of them. The two sets of diagrams are for Spring tides, the highest (and lowest), which occur once every fortnight, and for Neaps, which are less powerful and come in between. The lines indicate the times at which the tide will change, in relation to the time of High Water at Hull. HW−2 for instance means two hours before High Water at Hull, and the timing of the latter is given in locally obtainable tide-tables or, appropriately, in *The Times* newspaper, in the section headed 'Weather'. For the record, Spring tides are assumed to be those giving a level of 8.2 metres at Hull; Neaps give 7.0 metres.

As an alternative to all this mathematics, enquiry from the keeper at the last lock, or at one of the adjoining basins or side canals can prove most helpful, especially on the Trent and Ouse where a canal link from Keadby to Selby bypasses one of the trickiest lower sections. Here reefs of mud become exposed at low tide. A grounding in such territory can be quite serious, as the strong current pushing against light boats stuck on the bottom can cause them to heel over, while the banks often slope steeply and are sometimes stony.

The particular hazard of the Trent is the 'aegre', a local term for a tidal wave, which summarily introduces the incoming flood. This only materializes at the higher Spring tides, and may be affected by wind, or exceptional quantities of fresh

The 'aegre' or tidal wave on the Trent.

water flowing down. Similar waves or bores occur on the River Parrett in Somerset, on a section of the Severn that is bypassed by canal, and in several Continental estuaries.

The aegre can vary between being a barely noticeable slope, to something like a roller coming up a beach, and although easily negotiable by those who are prepared, it might be awkward, possibly dangerous, if met on a corner, or when lying near the bank. More significantly, the current changes abruptly as it passes, and further progress downstream may prove impossible. If attempting to enter one of the side basins or canals, it is usually necessary to let the current change first, in order to provide sufficient depth of water in the lock. Before entering one of these locks turn into the current first and stem it slowly, coming into the side, if needs be, to ask for advice. A dash across the current is always imprudent, with a risk of being swept against one of the entry piers.

Anchoring

Good 'ground tackle' can be the salvation of a boat broken down. It also provides a means of waiting through a foul tide.

Too frequently the anchors carried are small and the cable inadequate. A CQR or plough anchor of 25 lbs will suffice for small craft up to 30 or 35 ft long, in these conditions, with progressively larger sizes up to 50 lbs, the heaviest that can be man-handled, for barges and similar craft. These weights also apply to anchors of the Danforth type, or similar, but if the traditional Fisherman type is used – the sort that features in sailors' tattoos – twice these weights are necessary. The cable should be gal-

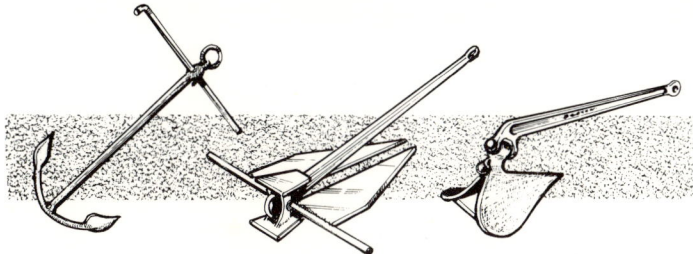

Types of anchor: from left to right, the fisherman, and the more practical Danforth and CQR or plough.

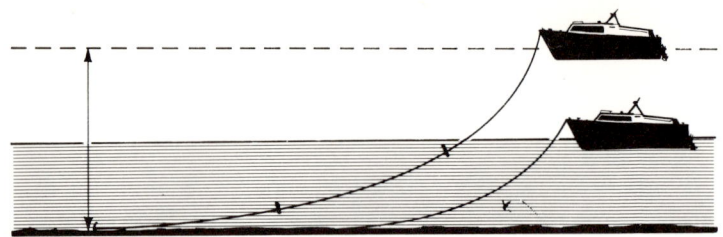

Plenty of cable must be allowed: with chain, at least three times the depth, allowing for tidal rise; with rope, many times more.

vanized chain, $\frac{3}{8}$ in being suitable for 35 footers, $\frac{1}{2}$ in thereafter, and since at least three times as much chain must be lowered, as the maximum expected depth, carrying 15 fathoms (90 ft or 30 m) is not being unduly pessimistic. Rope may be knotted to the end of this chain, and can sometimes replace it altogether, but a far greater length is then required, say six or seven times the maximum expected depth, allowing for tidal rise.

The ideal is to have the anchor on deck, neatly tied down with coherent knots in pieces of light line. The cable leads below through a chainpipe, but any arrangement will do, provided that the chain is enclosed so that it cannot accidentally spill overboard; and also that it can run out freely, and be quickly freed if it jams; and, essentially, with the inner end secured, usually with a strong piece of line that can be cut should the anchor be irretrievable and have to be abandoned, perhaps in a hurry.

Anchoring is something of an art, best accomplished with the boat turned into the current, and the anchor systematically lowered over a roller fairlead on the bow as the boat becomes stationary and then gradually drops back. All of which is easier said than done, but it pays not to hurl it out in a dangerous tangle, to avoid dropping it in a heap, or dance upon the whizzing chain in a vain attempt to stop it. A turn should be taken on a cleat or preferably a samson post in good time, and further chain can be let out under control. It is vital to secure the chain in a manner that can be undone again. Repeated turns and figures-of-eight are the normal answer, made with the unused tail of the chain, *not* the standing part – the portion between boat and anchor that will come under strain.

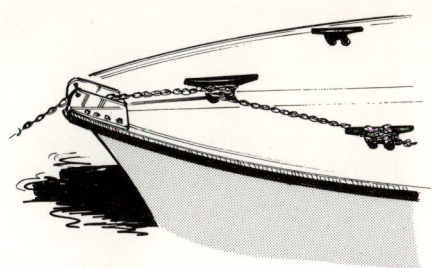

A roller fairlead prevents chafe.

If there is no roller fairlead, precautions will be necessary to insulate against chafe where the chain passes over the deck. It is also necessary to stand by for a few minutes to ensure that the anchor takes the strain properly and the boat maintains her position. After the pull has straightened out the cable, a dragging anchor may be detected with a hand upon the chain, or by observing marks on the shore. The solution is to let out more cable, or to pull it right in and start all over again – something that experts do quite often.

In making fast, it is dangerous to use the 'standing' part of a cable around a cleat or samson post. If the chain pulls tight it may prove impossible to undo.

The customary warning

The foregoing gives but the barest indication of seagoing practice. It cannot be stressed too firmly that the wider estuaries, such as the Humber, the Wash, Morecambe Bay, the confluence of the Thames and Medway, and the Bristol Channel outside Sharpness must all be regarded as sea passages, with all that this involves. All can display a mirror-like calm, but this is a dangerous lure and trouble awaits the unsuitable and unprepared. Narrow boats particularly qualify for these strictures.

Wider waters – the Continent

The Continental waterway system is huge, varied, significantly deeper, financed by the respective states and often free of charge to pleasure craft. Its success is largely based on its importance in carrying goods. The notion that freight on waterways is an outmoded concept is demolished by the constant improvements to the major routes, the construction of new canals, and by the vessels that ply. Four barges coupled together and pushed by a tug can take 10,000 tons at a time up the Rhine to Switzerland; elsewhere 1000 and 2000 tonners are widely used; but 350 tons is still a common capacity, with locks to suit, and there are hundreds of miles of tinier waterways interlaced, many of them highly stimulating

France has an extensive system, misleadingly easy to underestimate on the map. It takes at least three, preferably four, and for those who like to look around a decent eight weeks to travel from north to south by boat. Big rivers play a part, but the central canals are most varied and beautiful, with plenty of locks and a modest barge traffic. All locks are keeper-

On the Canal du Midi in Southern France.

operated, but, unless they are electrified, crews are expected to lend a hand. In summer locks open at 6.30 am and continue to 7.30 pm, with a half-hour break for lunch. At tunnels, which can be long, traffic is controlled and sometimes towed through with chain tugs or electric locomotives.

Locks measure 38.5 by 5.20 metres for the most part; depths are 1.80 metres or more. Exceptions are the picturesque Canal du Nivernais in the Centre, the Midi linking the Atlantic and Mediterranean in the south (30 metres by 5.25 metres, with low bridge clearances), and the comparatively neglected canals of Brittany. By British standards locks are fairly fierce, the range of paddle designs awe-inspiring (including some that wind down for opening). The bigger canals and rivers can be vigorous.

For a more detailed picture see *France – the Quiet Way* (J. Liley, pub. Stanford Maritime).

Belgian waterways are somewhat on the French pattern, but with fewer locks and longer hours. Traffic can be heavy on the broader routes, such as the Albert Canal, the Brussels–Charleroi and the new link between Antwerp and Holland, but an

Holland – 900 ton barge under way.

ancient line of canals inside the North Sea coast is comparatively lightly used, and provides a convenient access to the Netherlands.

German waterways are busy, often dramatic, and well controlled. The Dortmund–Ems Canal, for example, has a lower as well as an upper speed limit to regulate the constant traffic. The Rhine is staggeringly busy, despite its strong current; but the Moselle, unnavigable until the 1960s, has plenty of room to spare and is breath-takingly beautiful. Small self-operating locks are placed alongside the bigger chambers, and work by pressing a button. A difficulty on all such waterways is finding a safe haven out of the wash, and pre-planning is called for.

In Holland the heavy traffic persists, but may be escaped down hundreds of by-ways. Excellent maps, available locally, indicate depths, bridge heights etc. on a network of canals, rivers and lakes that might take a lifetime to explore. Formalities are minimal, likewise charges, though lift bridges, which are frequent, occasionally require a one-shilling tip. Safe mooring at the centre of a town is a commonplace, and houseboats are not despised. The Dutch themselves take to the water in their thousands, and fortunately have room to do so. On lakes and estuaries there are many sailing craft, and the motor boats

Holland – moorings in Dordrecht.

used are beamier than their British counterparts, often with a bluff bow that permits more room inside, and frequently built of steel. Such vessels indicate the basic requirements of the Continental system: something stable and tough, with rather more power, since some of the lakes and rivers get considerably rougher than the waterways in Britain.

Documentation

Unless hiring overseas, the following documentation may be necessary for visitors to the Continental waterways. A Certificate of Registry for the vessel, or alternatively an International Certificate for Pleasure Navigation, obtainable with less difficulty from the Royal Yachting Association, Victoria Way, Woking, Surrey. It is valid for two years. From the details thereon a Green Card will be issued, free of charge, by the Customs authorities upon arrival in France. This permits craft to stay for six months in any calendar year without importation fees, although in practice vessels may be left under a Customs seal and used again for six months in the year following.

Also necessary, for all countries, is an insurance document verifying Third Party cover on Continental waters, and for France in particular, a schedule of *chômages* (stoppages for canal repairs) provisionally issued in January and confirmed in March each year.

At the time of writing no licence charges are demanded of British visitors to France, although there are occasional fees for towing through tunnels etc. In Belgium, a ticket will be issued at the first lock or frontier point, costing something in the region of $12\frac{1}{2}$ pence. This covers a voyage through the country. In Holland there are no licence charges: likewise in Germany, although individual levies are made at locks, and a host of regulations *may* be brought to bear upon vessels greater than 15 tons displacement.

Arrangements can change, and in every case it is useful to verify with the respective tourist offices in London shortly before starting a trip.

Hulls and Superstructure

Boatbuilding and major repair work demands skills beyond the scope of many amateurs. Sound professional advice is worth having on many of these matters, particularly if buying second-hand, and most particularly if the vessel is made of wood.

If a surveyor is employed, purchase can be 'subject to survey', in which the price is agreed, subject to the surveyor not uncovering defects beyond those already acknowledged. The hopeful buyer pays for the survey and its associated costs (which can be considerable). In the case of large boats which cannot be hauled from the water, he will have to locate a dock, or a grid out on the tideway, and barter with those who appear to permanently occupy these rare facilities.

Surveyors vary in disposition and outlook. Some good ones are unqualified, but a list of qualified members can be obtained from the Yacht Brokers, Designers and Surveyors Association of Orchard Hill, The Avenue, Haslemere, Surrey. Be wary of anyone suggested by the vendor, and enquire a surveyor's fee and expenses before starting, making clear the limits of the proposed investigation.

With fibreglass hulls a surveyor can advise on any outside defects, but has limited means of assessing the quality and care of construction save by the reputation of the moulders and eventually knowledge of other boats in the class. With iron or steel, the traditional means of inspection is by drilling the hull. The process is a lottery, unless the vessel is riddled like a colander, and it causes permanent damage, however much care is taken in welding up the gaps again. At all costs avoid having holes burned, since this oxidizes and further weakens the plating. A few surveyors, such as M. G. Duff of Chichester, carry ultrasonic thickness testers.

Examining an iron boat from inside the hull, using an ultrasonic thickness tester. Note the buildup of scale or corrosion on the plates to the right of the picture. Despite its impressive proportions, the hull remained basically sound at this point, with some $\frac{1}{4}$ in thickness of solid metal remaining.

Timber

Traditional yachtbuilding methods are the province of the craftsman. The commonest forms are *carvel* construction, in which the hull planks are laid edge to edge to give a smooth surface, and *clinker*, in which they overlap, as in many an old ship's lifeboat. The best materials are among the most expensive: oak, mahogany, teak, pitch pine (now virtually unobtainable), and latterly a range of African hardwoods. Fastenings are brass or preferably bronze screws, copper nails, or copper or bronze rivets.

The internal hull members are either steamed, or cut with

85

regard to the grain and shape of the original tree. It is all very elaborate, and usually expensive.

Plywood construction is much simpler, the sheets being assembled in a box-like form, glued and screwed to a basic internal structure. The system had a comparatively brief vogue, but survives in decks and superstructures, while plywood remains in extensive use for internal partitions and fittings.

Traditional narrow boat construction employs 2 in oak planking on the sides, and untreated elm on the bottom, laid transversely. An oak keelson runs internally down the centre of the boat to provide a spine, and there are often steel right-angle frames or *knees* to which both bottom and sides are bolted. 'Composite' boats have steel sides, and the bottom planks are bolted to a flange. Timber-sided boats are lined internally by vertical oak planking, known as *shearing*, which is laid on brown paper, plastered with a tar mixture. The external planks are caulked, in a similar manner to carvel-built yachts, but in a cruder style, using *oakum* or loose hemp strands, which are afterwards tarred. The elm bottom is left untreated and will last for decades, provided it is not allowed to dry right out.

In all these craft a range of hazards is presented: cracked or split planking, 'nail sickness' (softening of the wood caused by corrosion of metal fastenings) and, particularly, rot. The search cannot be too thorough, and on narrow boats especially, old iron fastenings create a wealth of trouble. It is often possible to illustrate decay by wriggling with the fingers around the edges of iron knees, while the common practice of reinforcing bows with small overlapped iron plates often conceals deterioration. In many cases rot is revealed by judicious prodding with a spike or knife.

All old working boats are subject to distortion, which is best checked in the water, since they often resume their former shape when settled in a dock. A look down the sides will detect bulging, sagging, or more often 'hogging', a reverse sheer (ends lower than the middle, like a hog's back) frequently caused by moving the engine sternwards at some stage. Equally important is a check on the beam or width, which should be made across the bottom as well as across the top of the hold. Some narrow boats have spread with age, others were built slightly wider to take advantage of generous clearances on a particular canal;

but anything over 7 ft 0 in will stick in a lock sooner or later.

If buying a vessel as a houseboat, it is vital to check that a residential mooring can be obtained, and to consider the limitations of a high or boxy superstructure, which may come down like a pack of cards if the boat is ever moved and scraped against a curving tunnel roof.

Though pitfalls exist in plenty with 'yacht' construction, the common use of non-ferrous fastenings and the comparative youth of the structure slightly reduces the likelihood by comparison with aging and much-abused working craft. Clinker boats are prone to splitting at the *lands*, where the planks overlap, and they should not require caulking. Prolonged drying out will cause the timbers to shrink and open; systematic

A clinker-built converted lifeboat on the Bristol Avon.

dampening might close them again, but with carvel hulls the caulking may have dropped out. Replacing it calls for some skill, in making sure that the caulking cotton is not driven in too far, and is expensive. It incidentally provides an opportunity for treatment with Cuprinol or a similar wood preservative, if necessary. Such preservatives rarely penetrate far without application under pressure, and any rotten timber should really be removed, together with a substantial region of sound wood around it. Patching can be with scarphed or butt-jointed planks, overlapped inside the hull by reinforcement pieces glued and screwed in place.

Plywood is vulnerable at the edges, or wherever the surface has been scarred, and delamination can result, particularly during frost. All edges should therefore be well protected, and this is the general demand with all timber boats: careful maintenance, with frequent repainting, usually every season.

Storage under cover can save much toil in removing weathered paint or varnish. If an awning is used, it must be arranged to permit air to circulate underneath and through the boat, at the same time keeping out rain and snow. The time-honoured method is to lay a tarpaulin over a long ridge pole supported on crutches. The cover is left open at either end, like a tent. The difficulty lies in securing it against the wind, and at the same time contriving ventilation.

The roofs of inland boats receive heavy treatment: walking, lying, leaps from the lockside, and scrapes with hook and shaft. All timber roofs are vulnerable to these assaults, and to expansion and contraction under weather. In times past proprietary decking compounds have been applied with optimism, but cracking and leaking remains a common fault.

Canvas is a traditional material for deck covering. Those not actually doing the job often claim that it should be laid on a gooey mixture of old paint, but a sticky tangle is the most likely result. A saner method is to clean and smooth all woodwork first, to prepare an even and grease-free surface, and then apply two coats of metallic priming paint. When these are dry, the canvas may be laid, using closely spaced copper tacks. Stretching it evenly can be difficult, and small bags of sand are sometimes attached to overhanging portions in order to pull the canvas straight. Any joints in the canvas must be overlapped,

A wooden superstructure with a canvas covered roof.

and the edges bedded down on mastic. Wooden battens then secure these areas. Once laid, two coats of waterproof undercoat are then applied, to be followed by a compatible marine deck paint.

Embossed PVC coverings such as Trakmark require a similar thorough preparation and priming. If wood preservative is used first, it must be of a type that does not conflict with the adhesives. Since the latter are generally of the 'impact' type, the most thorough pre-planning is necessary, with the sheets carefully cut to shape. Butt joints are possible, but the material usually shrinks slightly, and parts. Overlapped joints are preferred, secured with battens.

Fibreglass covering likewise requires an absolutely smooth and clean surface. A first coating of resin mixed with styrene may be followed by neat resin, a layer of chopped strand glassfibre mat, and then a woven glassfibre 'roving', but precise advice can be obtained from the firms advertising resin and glass supplies in boating magazines. Strand Glassfibre Ltd, of Brent Way, Brentford, Middlesex is one of several helpful companies.

Roofing felt, though much despised and hardly photogenic, has many advantages, particularly for houseboats. Cheap, and relatively easy to lay and patch, it can be bought in rolls, and large areas covered in a day, securing with battens at the joints. It tends to wrinkle and will wear under heavy use, but it can sometimes be protected with duckboards, and will stay watertight for many years. It should not be tucked under at the cabin edge, lest it retain water and engender rot.

A wide variety of laminated board is used for cabin sides, often with a metallic or waterproofed outer skin. The protection of all joints and exposed edges is an obvious precaution, using either glassfibre tape or battens, screwed in place over mastic. Plywood sheeting is satisfactory, provided it is carefully maintained, but simple hardboard is less so, being prone to cockling, even if damped on the inside surface 24 hours before laying. It can be difficult to paint, or to keep thoroughly waterproof.

Steel

Modern canal boats are of mild steel, and invariably welded. Older craft may be of iron, or some early steel of quite staggering durability. Riveted construction, once common on barges and narrow boats, is almost extinct, due to its expense. The complex shape of many early hull forms illustrates the great care once taken in marking out and rolling plates, and the lack of concern over labour.

The modern steel canal cruiser can still last for decades, and survive many knocks in the process. Commonly, $\frac{3}{16}$ in mild steel sheet is used, but $\frac{1}{4}$ in is preferable, and less likely to dent. Structural forms vary; most canal pleasure boat hulls have transverse girders of an inverted L-section, to stiffen the bottom, which is generally flat. Sides sometimes depend for stiffening on a folded flange at top and bottom edges, and occasionally a slight curvature in section; but longitudinal girders are usually employed, with the occasional fillet or frame. Sometimes the internal reinforcement is welded at a diagonal. No matter: the aim should be a strong box structure.

The commonest faults in steel waterway craft are inadequate reinforcement near the stern, where the engine will be mounted, and where rigidity is most important; and insufficient rubbing strips on the outside. There should be several at the bow, one along the gunwale or near the top of the hull sides, and one just above the waterline. If possible, they should also offer protection to pipe outlets or other skin fittings. A further strip is necessary around the *chine*, the edge where the sides meet the bottom.

Welding is generally competent, but it is worth checking for

The steel hull for a canal cruiser showing typical reinforcement. Bottom and side plating will be of $\frac{3}{16}$ in or preferably $\frac{1}{4}$ in mild steel.

wavy welds, or those containing blowholes, while a discreet prod with a screwdriver at any soft-looking section may reveal failure to de-scale before painting. Very thick welds, or those that are heavily built up, are in fact weaker, and can cause distortion. Edge-on joints between different thicknesses of plate can also be vulnerable, and so too are heavy clusters or concentrations of weld, which develop residual stress.

Steel superstructures are usually of thinner material, commonly $\frac{1}{8}$ in sheet, in the interests of expense and stability. The roofs are curved for strength and reinforcement is often of square-sectioned tube, passed through a bending machine. Since this is inevitably laid face-on to the roof sheeting, and since it is difficult to seal all sides with weld, corrosion is inevitable in time, and some type of ridge reinforcement would be better.

If a steel boat has been in use, it pays to dock her, or lift her from the water, and to watch for any welds that are slow to dry. Examination with a de-scaling hammer will then reveal a failed or faulty weld, which should be renewed. Old working boats are often badly worn under the stern, particularly at the starboard or 'right hand side', where they will have rubbed the bottom most. Other vulnerable spots may be around the bow, on and just under the waterline. It is possible, sometimes, to judge thickness variation by clouting with a hammer, but curvature or the intervention of frames will demand a sensitive ear. Hard blows are necessary; if the steel distorts, it can be assumed to be $\frac{1}{8}$ in thick, or less.

Checking inside, and particularly close to frames or knees, will sometimes reveal thin side plates. If the frames themselves are corroded, it is a sign of general decay, and the hunt thereafter must be thorough. Early iron boats will sometimes corrode spectacularly, with the scale standing proud in heaps. In practice this oxide represents perhaps 100 times the thickness of the original plate that has gone to waste, and since these boats were often generously over-built, there may well be sufficient thickness remaining. The *SS Great Britain*, built in 1843 of Lowmoor iron, and for many years abandoned, had corroded less than half her thickness before being towed back to Bristol a century and a quarter later. Likewise, old barges often merit restoration, although a determined attack is necessary to stop scaling

An iron barge in dock for examination with the scaling hammer.

continuing; it should be chipped and wirebrushed right down to shiny metal, then painted with one of the patent primers sold by welding suppliers.

If renewal is necessary, the customary method is to lay a steel plate over the outside as a patch. Care must be taken to make the overlapped area completely airtight, and welds must be carefully checked; likewise the beam or width of the vessel, which can be increased embarrassingly by reinforcement on the sides. Technically, it is sounder practice to completely remove a corroded area and to weld in new plates, but the process is laborious and expensive, and careful overlapping will normally be sufficient.

Fibreglass

Glass-reinforced plastic (GRP) is the more specific term. Though still something of a mystery material, it has been used long enough to reveal certain shortcomings and has fallen slightly from the high standing it initially enjoyed. Its assets are low but not insignificant maintenance, comparative ease of production (provided it is in quantity), and the possibility of complexly curved hull forms that are harder to achieve in timber or in steel. The lightness of these boats also lends itself to trailing.

For inland use it demands careful fendering and protection with rubbing strakes, and a boat with a fibreglass hull needs a considerate owner. The material takes poorly to impact or abrasion, and a boat squeezed hard can be seriously damaged.

Its greatest success on waterway craft has been in superstructures, and it is possible to buy these, virtually by the yard, for rapid installation on a steel hull. Such roofs have a constant section and are sometimes supplied in two units for bolting end-to-end through flanges and a soft foam gasket, which is after-

A fibreglass cruiser with imitation 'clinker' planking, which imparts greater rigidity but demands careful moulding. (Robert Shopland, *Waterways World*)

A fibreglass superstructure mounted on a steel hull.

wards 'glassed' over inside. Some embody sandwich construction, with reinforcement in the form of a foam core that
neatly meets the problem of condensation. Fibreglass sheet and
foam sandwich is also used in the manner of plywood and laid
over a timber skeleton. The best roofs are those that flex the
least when jumped upon, and those sloping sufficiently far inward to avoid the majority of bridge arches, the material being
particularly sensitive to this type of collision.

Construction of a GRP hull is within a mould, in which glassfibre fabric, either woven, or more commonly of random or
'chopped' strands, is carefully laid. A polyester resin is rolled
on and into the glass to bond and strengthen it, and several
layers are built up in this way. The methods of laying (lamina-
tion), the choice of materials and the time needed for curing
are still disputed – particularly by builders anxious to maintain
a high rate of production. Improper curing is a serious worry,
particularly since it is impossible to detect at the outset. Much
therefore hangs on a builder's reputation and conscientiousness.
His premises must be clean and orderly, there must be means

of controlling both temperature and humidity, which means a sound and draught-proof shed, with control equipment clearly visible, and one man should be in charge of mixing resins and catalysts, which are ideally measured on scales. Boats are best laminated with some speed, in order that the different layers adhere properly, but they should stay in the mould for at least 24 hours after laying up, and thereafter be moved and supported carefully, since the process of curing continues for several weeks, and distortion can be permanent.

Common faults are inadequate lay-up, with too much unreinforced resin, particularly in awkward corners, or 'dry' patches where the glass has not been thoroughly impregnated. Careful design will reduce difficult areas, and it is also preferable to use rope, rolled paper or foam as reinforcement, relying upon the box section created in the laminate for strength. Wood reinforcement, though often necessary, can raise stresses at its corners and edges (and in time may rot), and wherever possible the loads at these points should be spread; likewise the edges of bulkheads, which can sometimes be set into foam fillets, and then bonded over.

Repairs to fibreglass

The outside of a hull is protected by a thin unreinforced layer of resin known as the 'gelcoat', and it is here that many troubles arise. Knocks and scars or surface crazing (small cracks) make the material vulnerable to seepage and to further flaking, particularly during frost. It is important to deal with any scrapes or cracks at an early stage, preferably during fine weather and certainly in dry conditions. Repairing major damage is a job for a professional, but small, uncomplicated areas may be patched by the owner.

Individual scratches and small flaws should first be cleaned out with a sharp tool, then degreased with a sparing application of acetone, using a fine brush to penetrate the cavity. Filling is with a choice of materials: filled resin, pigmented resin, pigmented gelcoat, or epoxy putty, carefully following the maker's instructions. If working below the waterline, pigmented gelcoat is generally the most suitable, and if the scratch is deep, a resin putty should be used first, and then covered with the gelcoat.

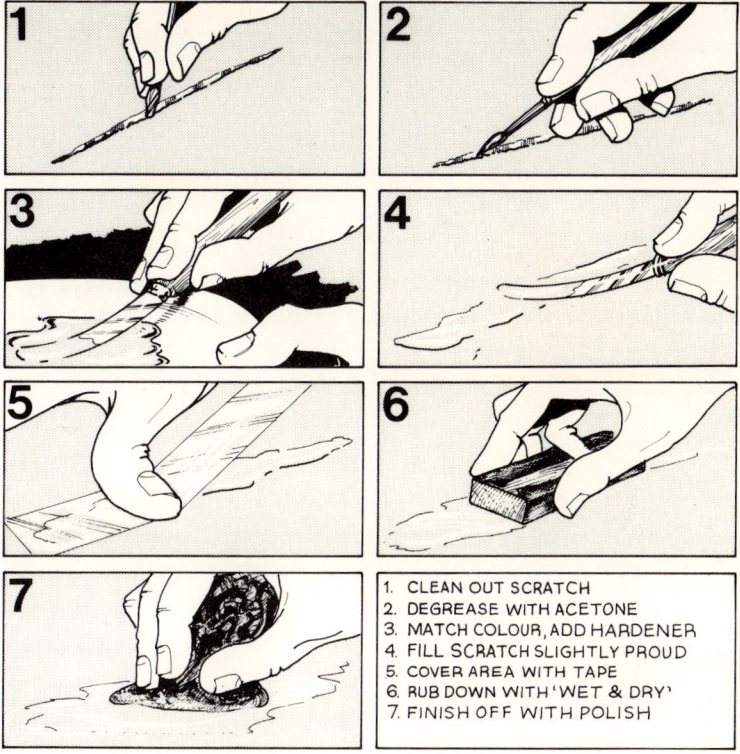

1. CLEAN OUT SCRATCH
2. DEGREASE WITH ACETONE
3. MATCH COLOUR, ADD HARDENER
4. FILL SCRATCH SLIGHTLY PROUD
5. COVER AREA WITH TAPE
6. RUB DOWN WITH 'WET & DRY'
7. FINISH OFF WITH POLISH

Air must then be excluded by fixing clear film or tape over the wet resin surface. The area is finally polished with a fine abrasive, once it has set and cured hard.

Multiple small scratches may often be treated by wiping sparingly with acetone, then sealed by wiping with resin. Very fine scratches can sometimes be polished away. Be wary of solvents which may damage the surrounding laminate.

Hair cracks, looking like a spider's web, may betray extensive damage. A dull response to a tap indicates the worst; in any event check within the hull and consider whether the damage has been caused by flexing. If so, consult an expert; if superficial, treat as before.

Deep gouges and small holes demand something of a rebuild. The damage is first trimmed right back, chamfered around, and then sanded, before washing and leaving to dry. With holes, the cavity is backed, preferably with a polished metal sheet, or a polythene surface to which the repair cannot stick. Roughly cut pieces of glass mat are then laid into place with plenty of resin, building up layer by layer. Once the cavity is filled it may be filed smooth, then sealed with two coats of gelcoat.

Uncommon materials

Other boatbuilding materials now in use are aluminium alloy and ferrocement. Aluminium is expensive, offers no particular advantages inland, and is unsuitable for repeated contact with *terra-firma*. Ferrocement, in which a non-porous concrete is plastered onto a dense steel and mesh frame, is currently being used to great effect in sailing circles, where complex hull forms have been produced in large sizes at minimal expense. Inland cruisers have been built from it, and the results have been mixed. The material will chip away from the reinforcement upon heavy impact, and stems have proved particularly vulnerable. It can be repaired with epoxy filler, once thoroughly dried out.

Ballasting

Many pleasure boat hulls are insufficiently ballasted, although with fibreglass a lack of weight at least minimizes damage upon impact. The penalty of lightness is difficulty in wind, but there are many instances where boats do not 'swim' well (a poor swimming boat in waterway jargon is one that is wilful and difficult to steer, whereas good boats are docile and tend to feel their own way along a channel). Getting the propeller deeper into the water, and sinking the rest of the hull down, can often overcome these problems, and experimentation will sometimes transform a boat.

The most popular ballast in steel boats is bricks laid onto bituminous paint. Other solutions are gravel in bags, concrete cast in lumps, or paving slabs. Iron castings are excellent, but expensive, and old railway fishplates are ideal, being much denser than concrete or stone. The ballast should not be able to shift or fall, particularly in wooden boats where it might start a plank. It must be removable in an emergency, and should leave a way clear for bilge water, and for rapid inspection of the bottom (for which the floorboards above ought also to be readily movable).

It is also possible to ballast a hull by pouring in liquid concrete, and in old working boats such as Thames lighters this has sometimes been done. The steel has to be de-scaled first and then painted, although some authorities prefer a light cement wash. The disadvantage is that the concrete shrinks slightly on setting, leaving a tiny gap for moisture; and of course the process is nigh-on irrevocable, and can make slipping or docking difficult.

Gravel is sometimes heaped directly onto a steel bottom, but unless it can drain rapidly, the inevitable condensation will cause corrosion beneath it and frequent inspection, ballast moving and painting may be necessary.

Cleats, bollards and rails

On fibreglass boats in particular, fittings are often too small, and there is a tendency to screw them into wooden reinforcement within the plastic moulding, rather than bolt right through using reinforcement pads on the inside. Cabin top handrails can sometimes be screwed in this way, if they consist of a wide low batten, since the pull on them is sideways rather than up, and there is comparatively small leverage; but all other fittings are best made as stout as possible, and bolted. Beware bronze, bow 'pulpit' rails that overhang, or fairleads with a narrow slot in which a line can jam. If outside rails can be avoided, life will be simpler in locks, and it is common inland practice not to have them.

For towing, or anchor work, a heavy attachment point is needed, centrally placed and with provision for taking chafe from the cable over the bow. A stout samson post is the ideal, passing right through the deck and attached to the bottom structure. In practice it is rarely provided, and a fiddly compromise results, with the cable wound round several cleats to spread the load, and leading through an off-centre fairlead, which will cause the boat to sheer in a strong current or wind. There is no substitute for heavy fittings, each capable of taking several turns, or figures-of-eight, perhaps with someone else's line, which may be several times thicker than normal.

Weed hatches

It is now common to fit steel inland hulls with a hatch above the propeller for easy access to weed, or that modern enemy, the polythene sack. In some cases the hatch is wedged down with a quick-release lever; in others it is bolted, often through a neoprene rubber gasket. In either case the flange is best arranged several inches above the water level, bearing in mind that excessive bilgewater or a gaping crew can sink the stern considerably. If bolts are used the hatch should be clearly marked, so that it is not rotated, and can be put back without risk of jamming.

Painting

With bare timber, clean the surface with coarse or medium glass-paper, then finish with fine. Dust, and ensure that the surface is dry. Give two coats of thinned metallic grey or quick-drying primer, then two of a compatible enamel or deck paint. For underwater surfaces use one coat of waterproof grey undercoat instead of the enamel, and follow with antifouling paint. At all times verify that paints used are suitable; epoxy or polyurethane paints cannot be applied over conventional undercoats or primers, nor should they meet other paints at a common edge.

For repainting timber, first wash the old paintwork and then rub it down with medium grade wet-and-dry paper, used wet. Rinse and allow to dry, then add two coats of enamel or deck paint. Underwater surfaces take grey undercoat, followed by antifouling paint. Primary stoppers and filling materials are generally best used over paintwork, i.e. between coats. They tend to shrink, and large areas have to be built up in stages.

New steel boats must first be allowed to weather, so that all the mill scale drops off. This is the blue-black finish, which usually survives for several weeks after delivery of the plates. Thereafter all rust and scale is removed, using grit-blasting, a rotary disc, or heavy work with a wire brush. Once cleaned down to polished metal, a wash primer is added quickly if conventional painting is to follow; but for hull sides and bottoms, on canals at least, it is better to forget the Cowes Week approach and treat them with black bituminous paint – the least revealing of inevitable scrapes.

The insides of hulls are often also treated with a bitumen compound, which is cheaper, less laborious, and in many cases more suitable than paint. Its disadvantage is renewed runniness when oily, and it can give people asthma. On the Continent, old engine oil is frequently used, put on with a paint roller, and the plates seem to last for ever. The disadvantages here are smell, and if the bilges are pumped, pollution, although Dutch barge-masters pump out into an oil drum, for collection at special depots.

Steel superstructures are often something of a showpiece. Paint manufacturers urge treatment with marine epoxy primer on top of a first coat of wash primer; two coats of acrylic enamel follow. Simpler, less technologically sophisticated paints are available, but beware 'red lead', the traditional first coat, since this is unstable, and gives poor adhesion for paint coming later.

If repainting steel, rub down and fill, using wash primer on bare surfaces, trowel filler on existing paintwork for any cavities, then two coats of enamel. If burning down to bare metal, beware the tendency to conduct heat right through and to remove paint from the cabin interior as well!

Fibreglass boats have to be degreased (even if they look clean) with detergent, or special cleaning fluids from paint manufacturers. Success may be judged by the even wettability of the surface with water. The surface is then sanded with medium wet-and-dry paper, used wet, to give a key, at the same time taking care to keep it free of finger marks. Once it is dry, a marine epoxy primer is applied, to be followed by two coats of acrylic enamel, two of polyurethane, or deck paint. For underwater surfaces use marine antifouling, over compatible primer or undercoat.

Ferrocement hulls are usually left to cure for two months or more after construction. Thereafter an expensive treatment in epoxies may follow, but chlorinated rubber paint is reportedly as good.

Traditional painting

Painted roses and romantic castles decorate many narrow boats. Their origins are much discussed, and attributions range

101

Traditional rose painting on a narrow boat.

from connections with Bohemia to the suggestion that the Duke of Bridgewater's first canal terminated at Castlefields, Manchester. Roses are to be found at Hinderloopen in Friesland, painted in a similar style, and the decoration is really in the broad tradition that embraces farm carts, traction engines and fairgrounds. Professional painters may be hired at many points on the English canals and will do the equivalent job. Those wishing to have a go themselves should buy a set of enamels, and also a set of brushes, one for each colour. For roses a pointed brush of reasonable quality will do the base discs, pointed No. 8 sables the petals, and No. 3 sables the stamens and veins of the leaves.

The preliminary stage is to paint a disc wherever a rose will be. White roses require a pink disc, yellow roses brown, and for red roses a mixture of red and black. Each disc is then shaded, perhaps with a touch of black, or red. Leaf shapes follow, painted around the cluster of roses, in green, and these too are shaded at the centres, using brown paint, while the green is still wet. Everything is allowed to dry, then the petals of the roses are flicked on, each with a single stroke of the brush. The stamens at the centre of each rose are accomplished with a couple of tiny dashes, using a slightly thinned mixture of white and yellow, and the leaves can be given rudimentary veins in the same manner.

Needless to say, some practice is necessary, and good rose painting is accomplished with speed and confidence.

Corrosion and skin fittings

In fresh water, rapid corrosion of steel hulls and fittings is most unlikely, although there are legends, unsubstantiated, of venomously polluted or saline waterways in which the material disappears before the owner's eyes. If in doubt, sacrificial zinc anodes may be fitted near the stern bearing, on the advice of the suppliers (usually M. G. Duff of Chichester). Given reasonably frequent inspection, with lifting out or docking for painting say every two or three years, inland boats should survive without such intensive precautions. Salt water yields a different story, and mild steel boats must be properly protected, or better still, not kept in it for more than a few weeks.

Mixtures of metals are always somewhat doubtful, anywhere. Bronze is reasonably secure, but brass or aluminium stopcocks or skin fittings may be vulnerable. Wherever possible, they are best placed above the waterline, and inspected from time to time. It is tempting to use plastic skin fittings instead, but the cocks sometimes swell and jam, while the outlet itself, a threaded pipe end with an outside flange, is vulnerable to biffs and swipes, and can shear off completely through scraping against lock sides.

Engines

Many inland craft are over-powered, in some cases so seriously that they have to totter around at little more than tick-over. Consequently, the initial expense is higher, there is greater inefficiency, greater fuel consumption, heavy vibration and less reliability. The only virtues are a slight advantage in stopping quickly, often nullified by choice of propeller, and in any case largely dependent on foresight; and a fractionally higher speed out on open water. In practice an increase in power gives a disproportionately small return on smooth water, and it is hull form, and in particular waterline length, that determines the maximum speed of which a boat is capable.

How much power?

Theoretical power figures to achieve 4 knots in smooth water are:

> in a 20 ft vessel, drawing 1 ft: 1.0 hp
> in a 40 ft narrow beam vessel, drawing 2 ft: 3.0 hp
> in a 70 ft narrow beam vessel, drawing 2 ft 6 in: 3.6 hp

In addition allowance must be made for transmission losses, and alternators, pumps etc. run off the engine, while a reserve is necessary for any current or handling in a wind. In practice, the following manufacturer's brake horsepower (b.h.p.) ratings leave an ample reserve for canal and river use in Britain:

> for a 20 ft light displacement cruiser: 5–8 hp outboard
> for a 40 ft steel canal boat: 9–12 hp inboard
> for a 70 ft traditional narrow boat: 10–15 hp inboard.

On wider waterways, such as lakes, estuaries or the truly wide rivers of the Continent greater power can be most useful in over-

Over-powering with an outboard, demonstrated by a dragging hull and heavy wash. The fuel consumption will be excessive, and this particular unit is in danger of being swamped.

coming a chop, but waves of such dimensions will not be encountered on non-tidal waterways in England, and power in excess of these figures will be entirely wasted.

Cooling systems for inboards

The basic woes and virtues of the different types of motor are covered in Chapter 4. Inboards are the more reliable, but can be difficult to fit in small, lightly constructed hulls. Beyond 25 ft, however, they must be the first choice – finance permitting.

With inboard marine engines, the principal difference from road use is in the transmission and the system of cooling. The car radiator is unsuitable, and quite elaborate water systems are sometimes called for. In the simplest case 'raw' water is drawn straight from the river or canal and circulated round the engine and exhaust manifold. The difficulty with raw water is its tendency to silt up the cooling channels, while the inlet itself can often block with mud or weed. A filter or strainer may be incorporated in the skin fitting and this can be withdrawn for cleaning, but the system has its uncertainties.

A typical diesel, showing extensive pipework added for marine use, with cooling water heat exchanger at top right.

The next stage is to use a heat exchanger, in which the engine heat is first absorbed by a closed fresh water circuit, then passed to a secondary flow of raw water. Another pump is needed, driven like the first by the main engine, and there are still the hazards of raw water although it is at least kept out of the engine block.

Alternatively, the engine water can be passed through pipes run outside the hull (known as 'keel cooling'), but these may be damaged in a shallow channel, and more commonly nowadays the engine water is merely passed through chambers welded inside against the hull sides of a steel boat. Only one pump is necessary, and this is often of the rotary type (such as the Jabsco) with a flexible neoprene impeller, driven by gear or belt from the main engine. There is also a header tank for topping up, and a bypass pipe and a thermostat. Occasionally there is provision for oil cooling as well, in either the engine or, more importantly, the reduction gearbox, if fitted.

Conversion kits are available for adapting road engines in this manner, but the majority of engines installed, and particularly diesels, are already 'marinized' by the manufacturers. Reliability, reputation, and availability of spares are the main considerations.

Air-cooled engines have an obvious attraction, but the disadvantage of noise. Installation must be as precisely specified by the manufacturer. The most important point is trunking the hot air away from the engine, and outlet ports have to be located where they cannot ship water. Putting them on a vertical surface within the cockpit sides is a popular and successful solution.

Some makes

In the marine world, makers' names are bandied about in the way that television sets were once referred to, or motor cars in the days before company mergers. Marine engine mythology is equally suspect, but here, in random order, are some common, or once common, makes of inboard engine seen on inland waterways.

Armstrong-Siddeley   A post-war attempt at air-cooling in working narrow boats; sometimes known as the 'potato-roaster', but successful on lighter loads with proper ducting.

Lister   The SR range has been enormously popular in steel-hulled canal cruisers, being simple, reliable and comparatively cheap. Hand starting is possible, and a definite 'plus'. The doughty JP 2, no longer made, is still available secondhand, with spares. Water cooled, it should be inspected by someone knowledgeable, lest, among other things, the cylinder liner seals have gone.

Kelvin, Gardner   Two famous makes, noted for care and reliability, and built specifically for marine use. Kelvin still do 10 and 20 hp units, at a price. Modern Gardners are too powerful for many requirements, though widely used in Holland. Secondhand models of early, smaller units repay a lot of trouble in overhaul and renewal.

Bolinder, Widdop   Legendary slow runners, built like the Tower of London. Started by blowlamp, gas jet or cartridge. It is said that a single cylinder Bolinder could make it back to base with an evaporated milk tin in place of the big end bearing – which gives some idea of standards of maintenance. Often worn out: for the skilled and passionate only. Continental equivalents, such as the earlier Kromhouts and the Blue Deutz, are still widely used, making the same splendiferous exhaust note.

Period piece: an early Bolinder semi-diesel with massive single cylinder, seen in a barge on the Grand Canal in Ireland.

National, Russell Newbery Favoured narrow boat engines of yore, once again worn. RN remains in business, in Dagenham, with a 20 hp diesel, among others; National are gone forever, and Sherlock Holmes is needed to find spare parts.

Petter In the canal business for many years, with ups and downs, from early blowlamp models to an increasingly popular present range. The PD units fitted in British Waterways narrow boats gave a lot of trouble, and as adapted industrial engines proved difficult to dismantle for repairs on site.

BMC A range of vehicle engines, adapted by Tempest Diesels of Stamford, Lincolnshire, with transmissions supplied by Newage of Coventry. Early petrol units, such as the four-cylinder Vedette (the basic Morris car engine), gave good service, and are still obtainable. The diesel Captain and Commodore sizes tend to be under-rated, perhaps because of gearboxes in times past, but now have the rugged PRM box, and others. Somewhat on the powerful side for canal use, but well adapted to the Broads and Continental waterways.

Perkins, Mercedes Similarly based on vehicle engines, but

properly adapted for marine use. Over-powerful for English canals, they are well suited for medium-sized boats on lakes or estuaries. The Perkins 4.108, with hydraulic transmission, has been widely used on bigger Broads boats and on the Continent. The old 25 hp P4M and others were used by the Admiralty with effect and can still be picked up, sometimes rebuilt.

Ford The petrol 100E and 105E car engines are favourites for conversion (see *Marine Conversions* by Nigel Warren, published by Adlard Coles Ltd).

Sabb, Volvo Penta and *Yanmar*, all imported, offer diesels of good reputation in the lower power range.

Outboards are perhaps best chosen on reputation and service facilities. Mercury are highly spoken of, but higher priced. Johnson and Evinrude produce identical engines, save in name and livery, and have given good service. Further reference is invidious; it pays to ask around, to avoid marques no longer in production, and most important of all, to choose a unit of *low* enough power to run healthily at normal travelling speed. (Selection and maintenance are discussed in detail in *Outboard Motor Handbook* by Nigel Warren, published by Stanford Maritime.)

Steam is making something of a comeback among enthusiasts. Attributes are its mystique and quietness; drawbacks complexity and expense. Engines tend to be purpose-built by such as Severn-Lamb Ltd of Western Road, Stratford-on-Avon, or the long-established marine engine makers, Stuart Turner of Henley-on-Thames.

Buying secondhand

Be wary: enquire carefully. Even 'reconditioned' engines are not always such, being sometimes bought in batches, checked arbitrarily, and resprayed. If possible, arrange for inspection by a skilled engine fitter, preferably from the original makers. Several manufacturers will perform this service, sometimes with prejudice since they prefer to sell new motors; but a cynical view can be worth having. The engine should be heard running. Ideally, checks should be made of end bearings, valve seatings, etc but this sometimes tempts an affray with the vendor, and your fitter's judgement will have to be taken.

Installation

An unfortunate tradition, handed on from salt water practice, is to install an engine on resilient pads. With fibreglass and timber boats there may be no option, but a steel hull offers the possibility of rigid mounting similar to that employed in barges and merchant ships all over the world.

Flexible mounting allegedly reduces noise and vibration, but brings a whole range of complexities. Since the engine itself is moving up and down, it demands two universal couplings (not one), and a sliding splined section in the shaft. These may be obtained from general engineering suppliers, who can also supply another theoretical necessity, a double conical roller thrust bearing. In practice, many universal couplings can transmit a limited amount of thrust, while a deep-grooved ball race will provide a satisfactory thrust bearing in small installations.

Thus, there is a lot of engineering work, and accurate

An air-cooled Lister diesel, solidly mounted on substantial steel bearers. The corrugated pipes lead away hot air. The cockpit floor is laid on channel girders, a neat touch that prevents water draining onto the engine.

alignment of the shafting and engine is still necessary. Other requirements are a flexible fuel line, not of plastic, and a flexible exhaust, using either stainless steel bellows, spiral-wound tubing (which cracks in time), or if the exhaust is water-injected, rubber pipe such as that supplied by A. N. Wallis of Greasley St, Bulwell, Nottingham.

The difficulty of these tasks explains the occasional enthusiasm for outdrives in the inland trade, and slightly reinforces the claims of the outboard, but an inland boat should not flex in the way that small craft often do at sea, and a solid installation should be quite practicable. With wooden hulls, and particularly with fibreglass, there is difficulty in providing a firm base, although girders can be laid on the timber, or timber-reinforced fibreglass, and bolted through. If this is done, it is important that the bolts themselves are not load-bearing, since they can chew into the softer material; and the stern tube bearing should not move in relation to the engine. A common precaution is to use a long shaft and a flexible coupling. This is *not* a universal coupling, and should not be used as such; it merely absorbs slight vibration and its usual construction is with nylon or plastic discs, bolted to permit a small elasticity.

Alignment

This is an awful job, hampered by inaccessibility, the weight of the engine, and the corresponding difficulty of moving it by minute fractions. If shirked, the result is heavy engine vibration, cracked engine legs, the shaking loose of small components, and wear in the gearbox, usually demonstrated by oil leaks through damaged seals.

Alignment is best undertaken with the boat in the water and fully ballasted. The holding-down bolts should ideally be a precise fit, but some engineers prefer them running in slots, with sideways adjustment done by means of packing or further bolts through metal tabs welded upright on the engine bearers. Adjustable mounts are available, ready made, but the common practice is to pack the engine legs with metal shims. The shaft coupling behind the gearbox is then checked with feeler gauges, noting any variations in the gap as the shaft is rotated. Axial misalignment is hard to verify, unless the coupling has a lip,

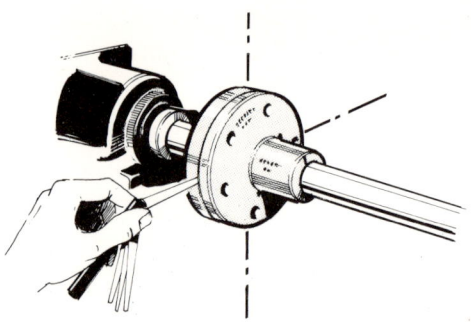

The theory of engine alignment: checking with feeler gauges. In reality, the coupling is never as accessible as this.

but if the coupling bolts are a tight fit, as they should be, it will be revealed with any angular differences at the coupling edge. Differences of say 0.002 in can be tolerated with the coupling turned through half a revolution, but much depends upon the length of shaft, and conscientious judgement.

Such measures are not always taken. That the breakdown rate on salt water is as small as it is speaks volumes for the low average time spent at sea. Pleasure boats on inland waterways often travel more hours in a week than seagoers do in a season, and errors in installation are all the more likely to show themselves.

Other points

A drip tray under the engine is advisable, and mandatory for wooden boats on the Thames; and the exhaust should include a flexible corrugated section, or a lengthy double bend to accommodate vibration. The Lister company of Dursley, Glos., thoughtfully manufacture silencers with standard pipe thread fittings.

A common fault with silencers is to mount them straight and low, with the risk that water may enter, particularly if the bilges fill, or the vessel is moored in a spot prone to wash. It is safer to lead it up high, with a final decline towards the outlet, but an air space is necessary if passing in the region of bulkheads or an overhead deck. Even if insulation is used, as much space as possible must be left, to minimize the fire risk.

A twin-cylinder Petter diesel with water cooling and 'manual' gear-box. Adjustment is through the small access hatch alongside the change lever, which looks long enough to inflict damage to the mechanism in insensitive hands. A hydraulic changing device would overcome this objection. The engine itself has, among other features, accessible piping, and hand starting with cylinder decompressors.

Marine gearboxes bear the same degree of unskilled examination as car gearboxes. In principle they are different — the marine box is 'epicyclic' — but in complexity they are much the same. They must be given the correct amount of the correct oil; adjusted occasionally, if there is scope to do so, by someone who understands the instructions — and otherwise left alone.

Some are manually operated; others have a hydraulic gear-change system powered by the engine itself. The latter is safer, for however violently the controls are handled they merely actuate a switch in the hydraulic circuit. With manual changing, pushing the lever forward engages a clutch; pushing it too hard can damage the change mechanism, sometimes a set of delicate toggles bearing against a pressure plate. Pulling the lever back

113

tightens a steel band around an enclosing drum, and this too may snap under extreme provocation. With manual boxes, both the band and the clutch can be adjusted to take up wear, a delicate job often made harder by the tiny access hatch.

Reduction gearing is frequently incorporated, either in the gearbox or a separate box, to reduce speed at the propeller shaft, but in some cases merely to alter the direction of rotation. It is vital to ascertain whether a 'left handed' or 'right handed' propeller is to be fitted, as the majority of gearboxes will quickly break down through taking thrust in the wrong direction.

Stern tubes

The outlet bearing for the propeller shaft is usually in bronze, sometimes with a patent rubber lining and water lubrication, but there are many possible arrangements. Sometimes the shaft passes through an angled shaft 'log' and then through a strut mounted on the outside of the hull; sometimes there are separate fittings inside and outside the hull, joined by an enclosing tube. In every case, however, there will be a 'stuffing box' or gland of some sort, to stop the water seeping in. This is a hollow section, reached from inside the boat by withdrawing a sleeve up the shaft. Packing material, usually a graphited flexible coil, is wound in a spiral around the shaft and then cut into rings with a stroke of a knife, preferably with the cuts at an angle. These rings are then pushed down inside the hollow section, and the sleeve screwed or bolted back in place. In every case

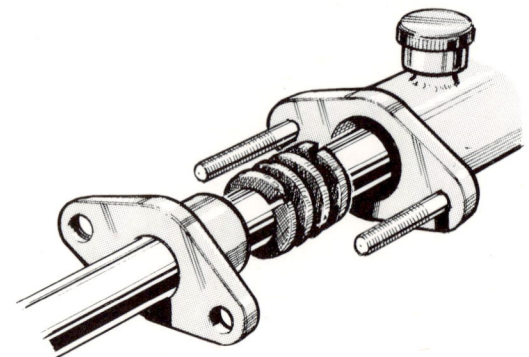

Typical stern gland, packing and grease cap.

the packing should be squeezed reasonably tight, but not hard, and lubricated with an occasional turn of a grease cap.

Worn stern bearings can be checked at the outboard end when the vessel is out of the water, usually by seizing the propeller and testing for sideways play.

Propellers

People devote their lives to the study of these, but the dimensions, at least, are fairly simple. Sizes are usually specified by the diameter, in inches, multiplied by the pitch and expressed in that order. The diameter is that of the outermost perimeter; the pitch the distance that the propeller would move forward, without slipping, with one complete revolution. It can be calculated by the mathematical by lying the propeller on a table, measuring the rise b of a blade, noting the width w at that point, and its distance r from the centre. The pitch is $6.28 \times b \times r/w$.

A 'right-handed' propeller, when looked at from behind or astern of the boat revolves clockwise in order to push the boat forward. A 'left-handed' propeller does the reverse. Propellers are nowadays usually in bronze for inboards, plastic or aluminium with outboards. Iron propellers are sometimes found on old working craft. Usually propellers are three-bladed, as a compromise between the heavier loading on a twin-bladed unit, and difficulties in design with four.

A damaged propeller can be a liability, not only in loss of performance, but in causing wear in shaft or gearbox, while changing size or pitch can sometimes transform a boat, giving the most efficient (and economical) thrust for a particular rpm/load/speed combination. Correct selection is as important for outboards as for inboards. Engine manufacturers will often advise, and also propeller suppliers, such as G. Spicer Ltd of Gaines House, Brent Way, Brentford, Middlesex.

Some years ago the magazine *Practical Boat Owner* published a most helpful guide, compiled by Nigel Warren, and a part of their table is reproduced here by kind permission. The following terms were used:

Velocity, in knots. This is not the speed of the boat, but the speed of water passing the propeller. Many boats to some extent draw water behind them. Those with bluff, squat sterns and the propeller tucked well underneath will do it most. For such a vessel travelling at 5 knots, the 'velocity' will be as little as three-quarters of the speed, i.e. 3.75 knots. For narrow boats with fine lines, it will be of the order of a $12\frac{1}{2}\%$ reduction, and for very efficient hulls, there will be a negligible departure from true speed.

DHP is the 'delivered horsepower', after allowance has been made for losses in transmission, power absorbed by an alternator or pump, etc. It is probably of the order of 90% of the manufacturer's figure for 'bhp' (brake horsepower).

RPM is the speed of rotation of the propeller. With direct transmission it will be the same as the engine speed, but if a reduction gear is employed it will be proportionately less. With 2:1 reduction, for example, it will be one-half, with 3:1, one-third the engine rpm.

By locating these figures in the table, pitch and diameter may be determined. A 'velocity' of 4 knots is as fast as most will ever need on inland waterways; in fact, even with a perfect hull it puts the boat some way above the general speed limit for canals. For most inland boats, a rudimentary approach will be to derive DHP at the maximum continuous engine speed, which is specified by the manufacturer.

A further column has been entered in the figures, that of 'efficiency'. This may be of theoretical interest only, but indicates what proportion of the power in the propeller shaft is actually turned into useful thrust. The original *Practical Boat Owner* tables extended upwards as far as 16 knots, but the figures below all relate to a velocity of 4 knots:

A simple example may be taken, that of a diesel developing 11.5 bhp at a maximum continuous running speed of 2400 rpm. The boat is a steel-hulled canal boat with some fairing towards the stern, giving, say a $12\frac{1}{2}\%$ reduction on true speed to obtain a 'velocity' of 4 knots. This represents a true speed of 4.57 knots, or 5.26 mph, as fast as this boat will ever need to go. We can therefore base calculations on the maximum power of 11.5 bhp, giving a DHP of about 10. Looking in the table, a range of figures is given for this DHP at a 4 knot 'velocity', with some nine different propeller sizes. The most efficient is the largest, with a diameter of 19.2 in and a pitch of 11.9 in, for a speed of 800 rpm. To use this propeller, a 3:1 reduction gear will

Velocity knots	HP	Prop. RPM	Per cent efficiency	Diam. in.	Pitch in.	Velocity knots	HP	Prop. RPM	Per cent efficiency	Diam. in.	Pitch in.
4	4	800	50·5	16·0	10·5	4	10	800	45·1	19·2	11·9
4	4	900	49·3	14·9	9·6	4	10	900	44·1	17·8	10·9
4	4	1000	48·0	13·9	8·9	4	10	1000	42·9	16·7	10·2
4	4	1100	46·7	13·2	8·3	4	10	1100	41·9	15·8	9·6
4	4	1200	45·7	12·5	7·8	4	10	1200	41·1	15·0	9·2
4	4	1300	44·9	11·9	7·4	4	10	1300	40·3	14·4	8·8
4	4	1400	44·2	11·4	7·0	4	10	1400	39·2	13·8	8·4
4	4	1500	43·5	10·9	6·7	4	10	1500	38·6	13·3	8·1
4	4	1600	42·8	10·5	6·4	4	10	1600	38·1	12·8	7·8
4	4	1700	42·2	10·1	6·2	4	12	800	44·3	19·9	12·2
4	4	1800	41·6	9·8	6·0	4	12	900	43·1	18·5	11·3
4	4	1900	41·1	9·5	5·8	4	12	1000	42·0	17·4	10·6
4	4	2000	40·5	9·2	5·6	4	12	1100	41·1	16·4	10·0
4	4	2100	39·9	9·0	5·5	4	12	1200	39·9	15·6	9·5
4	4	2200	39·2	8·7	5·3	4	12	1300	39·0	15·0	9·1
4	6	800	48·3	17·3	11·0	4	12	1400	38·4	14·4	8·8
4	6	900	46·7	16·1	10·2	4	14	800	43·6	20·5	12·5
4	6	1000	45·5	15·1	9·4	4	14	900	42·3	19·1	11·6
4	6	1100	44·6	14·3	8·8	4	14	1000	41·2	17·9	10·9
4	6	1200	43·8	13·5	8·3	4	14	1100	40·1	17·0	10·4
4	6	1300	42·9	12·9	7·9	4	14	1200	39·0	16·2	9·9
4	6	1400	42·1	12·3	7·5	4	14	1300	38·4	15·5	9·5
4	6	1500	41·4	11·9	7·2	4	16	800	42·8	21·0	12·8
4	6	1600	40·5	11·4	7·0	4	16	900	41·6	19·6	12·0
4	6	1700	40·0	11·0	6·7	4	16	1000	40·5	18·5	11·3
4	6	1800	39·2	10·7	6·5	4	16	1100	39·2	17·5	10·7
4	6	1900	38·7	10·4	6·3	4	16	1200	38·5	16·7	10·2
4	6	2000	38·3	10·1	6·2	4	20	800	41·7	22·0	13·4
4	8	800	46·4	18·3	11·5	4	20	900	40·3	20·6	12·5
4	8	900	45·1	17·1	10·6	4	20	1000	39·0	19·4	11·8
4	8	1000	44·2	16·0	9·8	4	20	1100	38·3	18·4	11·2
4	8	1100	43·1	15·1	9·2	4	25	800	40·5	23·1	14·1
4	8	1200	42·2	14·3	8·7	4	25	900	39·0	21·6	13·2
4	8	1300	41·4	13·7	8·4	4	25	1000	38·2	20·4	12·4
4	8	1400	40·5	13·1	8·0	4	30	800	39·3	24·0	14·6
4	8	1500	39·7	12·6	7·7	4	30	900	38·3	22·5	13·7
4	8	1600	38·9	12·2	7·4	4	35	800	38·6	24·9	15·2
4	8	1700	38·5	11·8	7·2	4	40	800	38·1	25·7	15·6
4	8	1800	38·0	11·4	7·0						

therefore be necessary. With a 2:1 reduction, that is with a shaft speed of 1200 rpm, a propeller of 15.0 × 9.2 in is listed, and so on.

BASIC ENGINE MAINTENANCE AND REPAIR

Two reminders, perhaps rather pompous, but born of bitter experience: follow the maker's handbook; and do not attempt too much. A skilled mechanic will often do the job in a quarter of the time and with much less damage. Marine engine attachments are often made in a relatively fragile alloy, and can crack or shear with over-enthusiastic tightening. Ring spanners in particular are best clutched well within their overall length.

Inboard engines

Routine overhauls: change the oil when specified, preferably while hot. Change the oil filter, then top up. Check belt tensions, and all greasing points; look around for leaks. In general it pays to keep an engine clean; it familiarizes the owner with it and helps him to notice faults. Detailed jobs, such as checking the cylinder head nuts for torsion (after running in, but thereafter rarely) should only be attempted with the right tools, in this case a torque spanner, or put into the hands of a fitter. Diesel injector nozzles can very occasionally be withdrawn and taken off for cleaning and checking at a lorry service centre, but they must be handled with care and reseated only after dusting round with a small soft brush. Jobs such as this, by no means skilled in engineering terms, probably represent the limit for the average owner with limited experience and resources.

Common faults (and it pays to look for the obvious)

Lack of fuel Is it on? Always turn the fuel off when finished with a petrol engine. Beware of doing so with a diesel: if the system runs dry, it will have to be bled to remove all air. Bleed screws are provided, usually on top of the fuel filter, and on the body of the fuel pump (the most complex part of a diesel). After slackening these in turn, fuel can be pumped through with the hand lift pump, if fitted, or by turning the engine on the starter. Retighten when air bubbles cease. (Then change your clothes and wash!)

Starter motor fails to turn: the cause could be a flat battery; equally often it is a broken circuit. Dismantle suspect terminals, particularly those on the battery itself. If copper, clean by immersing in hot water, then dry and reassemble firmly, taking care not to cause sparks or short-circuit the batteries.

Persistent starting trouble could be caused by short circuits, or cracks in leads, etc. Check belt tension to the generator, also the battery voltage regulator – usually in a small plastic box found by tracing the leads. A tiny layer of oxide on the contacts often inhibits charging and may sometimes be removed, after disconnecting the power, by wiping with an edge of paper. As in cars, petrol engines can suffer from short circuits in the plug leads, a cracked or dirty distributor cap, damaged points, etc.

Overheating: try the obvious once again, i.e. weeded or blocked inlets, failure to open the cocks, or simply lack of water in a closed circuit system. Slacken the pump cover briefly to see that water reaches it; in serious cases check through all pipework, and examine or test the thermostat.

Heavy vibration may be brought about by loose or cracked mountings, possibly by serious mechanical trouble, most probably by something caught on the propeller. Check by running in neutral.

Engine missing, running unevenly, or staggering: among the many causes the commonest is dirty fuel. It often manifests itself at the most inconvenient time, as when venturing across an estuary or going down the lower reaches of a river on a wild day. The cause is related: rust, water and sediment can lie dormant in the tank for years, but in waves will rapidly be shaken up. Some 80% of engine failures at sea result from this cause. The treatment is to clean or renew the fuel filters, then bleed the system. If venturing into choppy conditions, it is useful to know where the filters are, and to carry spares. The standard lorry-type filter, though adequate inland, requires a duplicate marine fitting in the line for seagoing, perhaps with a water separator as well. It should not be in plastic, nor should the fuel lines, in case of fire.

Engine running wild, caused by a broken throttle spring, or on diesels, an excess of fuel in the overflow chamber on the distributor pump. A drain tap or nut will be fitted and should be tended periodically. Very rarely a diesel will run wild on lubricating oil vapour. Get it into gear again, pull the stop lever (which shuts off normal fuel), and if desperate cover the air intake tightly with coat, hat or jersey.

Other faults – there are of course hundreds of possibilities, as with cars, and they provide profitable fields for keen mechanics. The non-ardent may be consoled that a reasonably maintained marine unit can run for years without idiosyncrasy.

119

Winter lay-up

Enemies are frost, condensation and damp, and acidity in used oil. The first stage with an inboard is to run it in order to heat the oil for easy draining or pumping out. Fresh oil is then added.

There seems to be no limit thereafter to the dismantling and injection of special fluids specified by manufacturers. Some advise disconnecting a diesel line, having turned the fuel cock off first, and running the engine briefly from a secondary tank, or a can containing an inhibiting fuel, with all the palaver of bleeding the system. General advice is to inject some lubricating oil into the cylinder head after removing the injectors (with petrol units the plugs), then cranking the engine over a single turn, before reassembling. It is also possible to tip a cup of in-hibiting oil into a carburettor while running, choking it to a stop.

Afterwards all inlets are shrouded with adhesive tape, electrics removed or covered, and terminals smeared with petroleum jelly. Petrol tanks must be drained, but diesel tanks can be left filled, right up to the top in order to reduce the volume for condensation. In draining water systems, the cocks and plugs on the engine itself can often be misleading, since they are not always at the lowest point. Start by turning off all outlet cocks and fittings; then drain the block and manifold, blowing through if necessary. Also, loosen all pump covers, and look round the cooling circuit for spots where water might settle. If antifreeze is used instead, it has to be circulated right round the system, with the engine warm, and checks made for small leaks, which this fluid is liable to find. The system will have to be drained and flushed through the following Spring.

Restoration, after the winter, is the reverse of laying up, but the bottom of a diesel tank is best drained off into a jar first, to remove silt and water. The fuel filter should also be examined and if necessary renewed, and a general inspection made.

Outboard engines

Mounting on a stout, well reinforced transom is important. If the engine is raised, hardwood packing pieces are best inserted in the gap between the top of the transom and the clamps. Correct mounting is theoretically with the engine cavitation plate (a horizontal, flat plate above the propeller) level with or just below the hull bottom and parallel with the water surface when running; but experimentation may be necessary. Many inland craft have a 'tunnel' in the hull near the stern, a concave portion which enables the outboard to be mounted higher.

Anti-theft devices are commonly fitted, usually as a hardened steel channel padlocked in position after sliding over the clamps. Though certainly a deterrent – save to determined thieves who saw through transoms – they can disguise loose mountings, and the clamps must be checked periodically. Losing an outboard overboard is a surprisingly common accident, and a safety line or chain, firmly attached, will reduce the agony of retrieval.

Engine lubrication will be specified in the handbook, with a gear oil change after running in (often after ten hours) and periodic replacement thereafter, coupled with routine oiling and inspection of screws and linkages. The following are common faults.

Lack of fuel – Is it on? Is the vent screw to the filler cap opened? Is the carburettor choke operating?

Too much fuel, caused by over-choking, or heavy use of the priming bulb that is often fitted with snap-on fuel lines. Symptoms are dripping and smell. Check further by disconnecting or switching off the fuel, then removing the plug to see if it is wet. If so, wait a little, then turn the flywheel several times with the plug out. Then try again.

Dirty fuel can gum up filters, clog the carburettor and affect the plug. Usually two-strokes, outboards require a fuel and oil mixture, thoroughly and accurately blended as specified. Do not use multigrade oils in the fuel blend, or leave old mixtures in the tank, as they can lose their more volatile (and ignitable) constituents, break down, and leave a residue. Tackle the carburettor warily, if at all, since settings are delicate, parts microscopic. Examine the filter at the fuel pump instead, and collect a little petrol in the hand, to examine for water, which is visible as globules or bubbles. If in doubt drain the fuel away into a can, then renew the filter.

Electrical failure: verify by disconnecting a lead, holding it close to the cylinder head (preferably with a glove or dry cloth) and at the same time spinning the flywheel. A strong spark

121

shows that the system is in order. If absent, look for loose connections, dirt, broken contacts, etc – or at the plug.

Plug failure: checked by removing the plug, reattaching the lead and spinning the flywheel with the plug laid on the cylinder head. If there is no spark or only a weak one, clean the contacts with a knife or emery cloth, and adjust the gap with a feeler gauge to the prescribed clearance.

Overheating can be caused by faulty fuel, a faulty carburettor, not enough oil, too much oil, etc. Try looking at the water circulation instead, or the water pump.

A fouled propeller is much more common, bringing juddering, vibration, or stopping the engine altogether. If a propeller shear pin breaks, renew. If no spares are available, a line wound round the central boss and blades will sometimes serve as a makeshift, as will a piece cut from a soft nail.

Generally, it pays to keep the engine working without overmuch idling; but throttle well down for gear changes. Running too cold seems safe enough, but means loss of power and high fuel consumption. When removing the engine, it should be kept upright if possible. If laid on its side, water can sometimes drain in through an open exhaust valve.

Dealing with a submersed outboard

Recover, dry, inspect the electrics, then remove the plug and turn the flywheel over several times. Add a little oil. Turn over again, then renew the plug and attempt to start. Repeat *ad infinitum*, but beware mechanical resistance to turning; serious damage is sometimes caused by immersion when running. If the engine can be restarted, keep it going for at least twenty minutes.

If in salt or heavily polluted water, first wash with fresh; then try to start. If necessary dismantle for an overhaul.

Winter storage

Flush by running in clean fresh water. Drain the tank, then run again to empty the carburettor. Drain water, clearing all holes and removing the drain plug. Renew gear oil. Add oil through the cylinder head, and to all linkages. Where possible, remove and dry the electrics, or cover. Store upright in a dry place.

Equipment and Systems

Fuel systems

Tanks are generally of mild steel, which should not be internally painted or galvanized, for fear of chemical action. They may also be of stainless steel, aluminium, or flexible nylon-reinforced rubber. Fibreglass tanks are somewhat dubious unless the correct resins are used, and particularly so at the 'higher temperatures found in an engineroom.

Important points in tank installation are even weight distribution, firm support beneath and for the sides, and the use of internal baffles to prevent the fuel from surging. Unless a tank can be mounted across the boat twin tank installations are more satisfactory for maintaining trim, with a large-bore connection to allow rapid filling. The filler pipe should be of a large bore also, of at least $1\frac{1}{2}$ in and preferably 2 in internal diameter, with a screw-down cap, clearly marked, located where it will neither take in water nor spill inside the boat during filling. The filler pipe is often led well down towards the bottom of the tank in order to reduce blowing back when filling; waterside pumps are sometimes fierce, and those on refuelling lorries especially so.

At least one vent is needed on each tank, leading upwards to a higher level, then turning over to a point outside the cabin or the coaming and arranged so that water and spray is not taken in. On the upper Thames, flame-arresting gauzes must be fitted over the ends of all vent pipes, whether for petrol or diesel oil. The mesh size specified has a minimum of 28 strands per linear inch, and the vent pipe must be at least *double* the bore of the engine feed pipe for tanks over 10 gallons.

The engine feed or supply pipe is most sensibly led from a point some way above the bottom of a tank, say 2 in, so that it will not take in silt, and there is often a recess or depression in the tank bottom in which dirt, corrosion and water may collect and be removed through a drain plug. Some authorities frown on tank drain taps, on the grounds that they might be accidentally knocked open, and a spanner-fitting connection is to be preferred. For similar reasons, engine sight gauges are doubtful, unless provided with a shut-off connection and a drain cock. Such an arrangement, though more accurate and reliable than a remotely connected dial, is not at all suitable for petrol tanks, where a car-type gauge will have to be fitted.

The engine supply pipe is best made of seamless copper, secured to the hull by plastic clips. Opinions differ on flexible connections: heat-resistant armoured hose is available, and is perhaps to be preferred, although some users bend the copper feed pipe in a large double spiral before connecting it to the engine. Chafe is the danger here, as the engine vibrates, or work-hardening of the copper, and in time the line can fracture at the connection union. This method should not be employed with petrol systems.

A fuel shut-off cock or tap is important, located as close to the tank as possible. Ideally it should be accessible from the steering position in the event of fire, but this is not always easy. It has been suggested that heat-sensitive valves, such as the Teddington Fire Protection Valve used in domestic oil appliances, will shut off supplies in the event of overheating. The classic problem is that the fire, fed by the fuel, may cut off access to the shut-off.

Fuel filter systems for boats are available from the Lucas/CAV group, who supply filters for sediment with replaceable paper elements, and water separators which can be fitted alongside. Plastic or glass filter containers or sediment bowls should always be avoided, for fear of melting or cracking. An aluminium casting is suitable, but making a connection can be tricky, since the casting may crack through over-tightening. Maintaining a fuel-tight joint is particularly difficult (and necessary) with a diesel, and patent jointing compound often washes off. Thin PTFE (Teflon) tape will sometimes do the trick, and the pipe fittings themselves, notoriously difficult to obtain from the average garage, may often be replaced by bottled gas unions made of brass, since they have the same threads.

Outboard motor tanks, often portable, are best placed in a locker, vented over the side. The snap-on connection, rather like a gas-poker fitting, should be fed back into the locker, over the top of this container, when not in use.

Electrical systems

Small craft depend on batteries, often similar to those used in cars or lorries: the familiar lead/acid type, and occasionally the expensive but durable alkaline battery. Batteries should be, but frequently are not, stowed in a secure box. This must be vented and yet protected, and close to the starter to minimize resistance in the leads. Cleanness is important. The cells should be kept topped up with distilled water to cover the plates, and may be checked with a hydrometer, a simple bulb and float device obtained from garages. A battery isolating switch, as made by Lucas, avoids accidental short circuits when away (but should not be operated with an alternator running).

Batteries thrive on use, with steady charging up to maximum capacity, and then gradual discharge. This is the sequence that should be provided during the winter lay-up.

Battery requirements can in theory be deduced by simple calculation. Watts = Volts × Amps. A 12 volt battery rated at 35 ampere-hours (AH) will yield 35 amps of current at 12 volts for 1 hour, or 1 amp at 12 volts for 35 hours, and so on. By adding up the power requirements (wattage) of different fittings the current drain (amps) on the battery can be calculated, and matched against the battery and charging capacity. In practice it is difficult to prophesy how long any light or pump may be used, and a trial-and-error approach is commonly adopted. Restraint is therefore necessary in adding extra fittings and such demanding extras as windscreen wipers and spotlights must be fitted with caution.

Circuitry should be laid out by a conscientious electrician, arranged out of the way of bilgewater, hatchways or areas of high condensation, and with junctions and fuseboxes at carefully protected positions. Avoid indiscriminate earthing, likewise deck connections, since 'watertight' plugs do not always remain so.

While 24 volt systems may be preferable, simple 12 volt circuitry has proved quite satisfactory on small craft without much elaboration. A separate battery and circuit for engine starting is a useful insurance. A blocking diode allows simultaneous charging, with the two batteries connected in parallel across the charger, and it permits separate discharge.

Generators

The simplest form of all is the DC dynamo, belt-driven from the main engine. This should provide for modest needs. Such fitments require little maintenance, other than tightening or replacement of the drive belt or new carbon brushes. They are best not interfered with otherwise. Alternators, because they involve electronic diodes, can suffer damage through interruption of the circuit while rotating. They are more expensive, even less suitable for amateur attention, but more commonly seen. Their advantage is high current output (AC) even at slow speeds.

Elaborate auxiliary generator sets are sold with great enthusiasm for luxury motor yachts, and they permit the use of electric cookers, fridges, washing machines, and so on. To mitigate the thundering roar, there is often a connection for a shore supply, when moored – but this facility is still rare on inland waterways. Portable generators are more often used, for battery charging and the running of small appliances. The common disadvantage is noise and fumes, and since many have four-stroke petrol engines, the presence of a highly inflammable fuel on board. Diesel units are also obtainable, but are correspondingly bulky and expensive.

Lights

Interior lights for boats come in many forms. The most economical (in current consumed) are those of the fluorescent type, although the 'frosted' cover commonly fitted slightly reduces their effectiveness.

Outside lights can include spotlamps of the most penetrating power – and high current consumption. For use on narrow waterways, a low-powered car or motorcycle headlamp with a *wide* beam will give illumination where most needed: against the banks, the sides of locks and the arcs of bridges and tunnels. Navigation lights for small boats are often badly screened and of insufficient visibility for use at sea. Inland requirements are less stringent (on canals, in particular, a solitary headlamp is normally considered sufficient) but proper lamps for heavily-used river navigations, or for estuaries, should be of high power, and screened to show red, green, masthead and stern lights in the correct sectors. In West Germany certain standards are insisted upon; navigation lights certified to these requirements are available from A. N. Wallis & Co of Greasley St, Bulwell, Nottingham.

Paraffin lamps, though picturesque, are difficult to trim and keep lit in the open air. They tend to blacken the glass, go out, or erupt in a ball of flame. For interior use they are often more manageable and also romantic, but should not be left unsupervised.

Gas installations

Bottled gas is sold under a variety of trade names, such as Calor and Camping Gaz. Unlike natural gas, this liquefied petroleum gas (LPG) is heavier than air, and can be difficult to disperse. It presents a considerable fire or explosion risk in enclosed surroundings, such as the hull of a boat.

The safest place for storage is outside the cabin, in a container deeper than the bottle itself, and vented at the bottom (through a hole in the vessel's side, if built into the hull). The internal diameter of the vent should be at least $\frac{1}{2}$ in for a 32 lb gas bottle, but preferably larger. A length of approved flexible hose (to BS 3212:1975) can be used to link the bottle and its reducing valve, but attaching the valve directly and putting the hose on the low pressure side can sometimes be safer. All these connections should be made within the container. Thereafter piping must be in solid drawn copper, led as high up as possible (and certainly not in the bilges), with a minimum of connections. If two bottles are used within the container, non-return valves are necessary to prevent leakage when a bottle is changed. Connections can be checked from time to time by brushing with soapy water (not by using a match), and gas

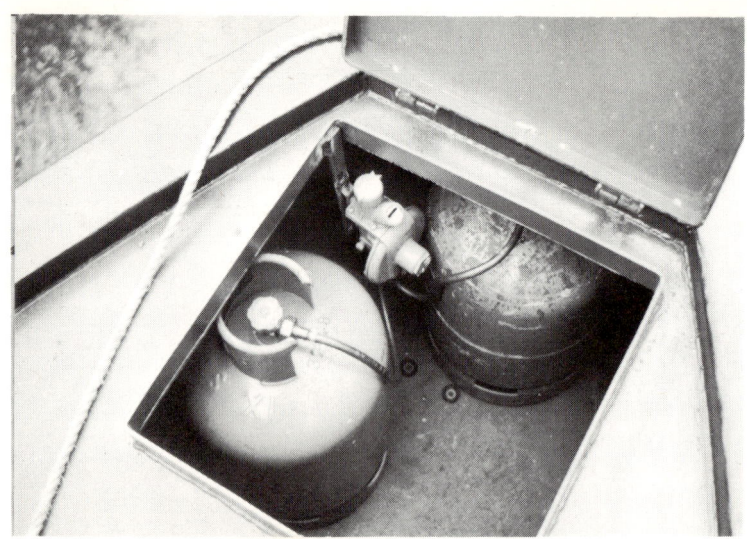

Gas bottles stowed in the bow of a steel boat. A bulkhead prevents any escape from reaching other parts of the boat, and small holes through the hull side will act as vents. Here flexible hose, of an approved type, is led to a pressure reduction valve, with a manual switch for changing from one bottle to the other.

cylinders are best turned off when not in use for any length of time. Proprietary 'sniffers' or gas detectors are available, for laying in the bilges; they should activate an electric alarm.

Bottled gas is lethal stuff, and the many precautions taken are justified. Small camping bottles are best changed out in the open air, well away from a stove or pilot light. If starting the engine after a long lay-off, it is sensible to sniff around the bilges first, lest the starter motor should ignite escaped vapour.

The larger bottled gas containers use a left-handed thread at the main connection – the opposite direction to the norm. If voyaging abroad, it will be discovered that several Continental containers are interchangeable with British makes.

Galley equipment

A wide variety of cookers, grills and ovens is available. Many are ordinary household units, adapted to the different pressure and calorific value of LPG. There is a narrower choice of gas-operated refrigerators, which tend to be small, and in some cases lacking in heavy insulation (refrigerators working from an electric compressor, such as the Canpa system from Camper & Nicholsons of Southampton, can be highly efficient, particularly if the cabinet is purpose-made with a top opening; but they are beyond the generating capacity of many small boats). Gas fridges must have a flame failure device, and it may be necessary to clean the flue occasionally. In waves, the pumping action in the chimney, caused when the vessel rocks, will put the flame out, and gas refrigerators are unsuitable for such waters. Other troubles can often be cured by laying the refrigerator on its back or by loading it into a van, and driving around for half an hour on bumpy roads.

Wall-mounted water heaters have an adjusting screw near the tip of the pilot outlet, reached by removing the front cover. In winter the whole unit must be drained, usually through a bolt hole below the flame system.

Heaters

'Catalytic' heaters running off bottled gas are now popular, being easily installed and working without a flame. They oper-

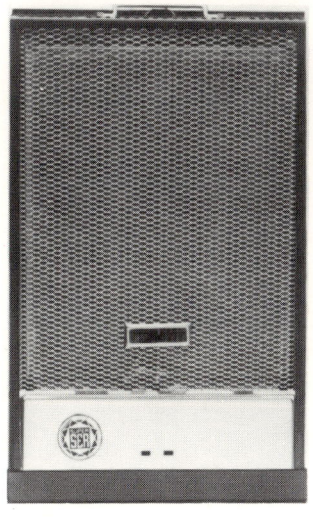

A 'catalytic' heater, the Super SER Panel 58, suitable for wall mounting and with a safety device for shutting off the gas if the system is interrupted. When working, such a unit emits considerable heat but will not ignite materials dropped against the element.

ate on the interaction of the gas with a permanent chemical catalyst within the grille, can be in contact with paper without igniting it, and depending on the surface area, have an agreeable heat output. Some must first be lighted with a match, but others have automatic ignition and, importantly, a safety device to prevent uncatalyzed gas escaping. Inevitably they require ventilation and, incredibly, they are sometimes installed quite high – a hopeless position for a heater with limited radiation properties.

Gas flame heaters often require a flue. Some, such as the Trumatic, an adapted caravan (trailer) heater from Carver

A solid fuel stove, installed in a narrow boat.

Engineers of Coppice Side, Brownhills, Walsall, have a facility for ducting hot air to different parts of the boat through spiral-wound tubing, with vent control at the ends.

Liquid fuel heaters are more complex, often being incorporated into cookers and water heaters, with electric pumping. Some work on a drip-feed system, others start in the manner of a Primus, with preheating by methylated spirits or a capsule. Boating enthusiasts are split on the matter of reliability; the output is often considerable, but there are occasional shows of temperament, at least when starting. The range of heaters and cookers by Perkins Boilers Ltd of Derby operate on diesel fuel through a pressure nozzle, with control by a photoelectric cell, and automatic re-ignition or cut-out.

Solid fuel heaters have made something of a comeback, and are certainly the most romantic. Much depends on safe installation, with a flue clear of the cabin lining, and penetrating the roof through a sheet of metal or a cast iron fitting that can disperse conducted heat. The stove itself is best mounted on a marble slab, or similar, capable of receiving hot ash, and backed by a reflecting or insulating surface. A chimney cowl may help (a beautifully made rotating type in the shape of a sphere is sold by Continental barge chandleries), so can a system of dampers, or a selection of shields that can be put across the face of the fire. Some household stoves have a gauze that can be slid in front, a useful precaution with driftwood, in particular, as this often spits and sends out sparks. As with most heaters, it is unwise to leave solid fuel stoves unattended, and important to arrange ventilation.

Fire extinguishers

A 3 lb dry powder type is common, but 10 lb or, better still, 20 lb extinguishers will be of far greater value. There should be as many as possible, prominently displayed and distributed around the boat and with comprehensible instructions. They need to be placed so that fire is not likely to cut off access to them, e.g. not behind a stove.

Fire-fighting really demands practice, which not many can have. Basic measures are to get close to the fire and to aim near and low. A common first reaction is to direct an extinguisher jet too high into the fire.

Dry powder extinguishers can be easily recharged. They may be used on electrical fires and have little effect on the user, although the powder will often billow back into the face, and does not penetrate behind fixed objects.

BCF, a gas stored as a liquid, overcomes this objection, and is particularly effective on engine fires, although it can be toxic in a confined space.

Carbon dioxide extinguishers, also effective, are heavy, expensive and difficult to check.

Carbon tetrachloride extinguishers are efficient, but because the fumes are toxic (extremely so where there is any alcohol in the blood) they are seldom installed today.

Various automatic detection and extinguishing systems are available, for installation in engine rooms or in an engine compartment. These sometimes suffer from over-complication; beware types involving a master switch, which might not be known to all crew members, or may even be inaccessible owing to the fire itself. Such systems should always be backed up by further hand extinguishers.

Also highly recommended: at least one bucket, for carrying water to non-oily or non-electrical conflagrations; an asbestos 'fire blanket' near the stove, although any heavy blanket or coat can be just as useful in smothering flames; and a continual awareness of the risks from escaped gas lying in the bilge, refuelling with the pilot light left on, and so on.

Water systems

A tank or tanks in the bottom of the boat, where they do not impair stability, are usual. Water may be pumped up by hand, but commonly a pressure supply system is used, maintained by an electric pump. Very occasionally a header tank system is installed, but there are natural limitations in balance and overhead clearance, as well as the necessity for frequent pumping up.

Hand-operated pumps, for cold water only, are useful in restricting the amounts that people use, particularly if they are unfamiliar with boats and assume that supplies are unlimited. They are now usually made of plastic or aluminium, and often have a small ball valve that can stick after a season's use (cautious application of vegetable oil will give temporary relief).

Tanks are generally of galvanized steel, plastic, or nylon-reinforced rubber in the form of a bag. They are said respectively to corrode, to make the water taste, and to rot, but the first is widely used in households; all benefit from complete renewal of water at regular intervals, and periodic flushing through. Estimates of size vary considerably, as individual use can vary between one and ten gallons a day – even more if hair-washing or baths are undertaken. A shower used in a leisurely fashion consumes on average 3–4 gallons each time.

Large tanks are best placed in a central position, or divided, with one on each side, in order not to impair the vessel's trim. Except for the flexible variety, they require vents, leading higher and taken to a point where they will not ship dirt, spilled fuel, or water used in washing the deck. It is useful to place them near the filling point, to provide a visual check when taking on water with a hose. The filler cap itself ought to be clearly marked and placed well clear of that for the fuel tank, to avoid a disastrous misapprehension.

Pressure systems have an electric pump drawing water from the tank to maintain a set pressure within the piping system beyond. When a tap is opened, a sensing switch within the pump brings it into action until the pressure is built up once more. If many taps are employed, pressure tank systems, such as those made by H. J. Godwin Ltd of Quenington, Glos., or the G. & M. Power Plant Co. of Whitehouse Road, Ipswich, are the more suitable. Such units maintain pressure within a drum-shaped container, and with this larger volume under pressure are not so sensitive to minor variations, cut in and out less frequently and cause less disturbance. On inland craft, however, the simpler and cheaper pressure pump system is commonly fitted, such as the Jabsco Aqua Maid from ITT Fluid Handling Ltd of Bingley Road, Hoddesdon, Herts. Such pumps are connected into a single pipeline, which can afterwards be divided, with one portion running through a water heater, the other leading directly to the cold taps. Two useful accessories are an accumulator tank, to give a greater reserve and enable the pump to operate with less frequent switching, and a cut-off switch to protect the pump should the supply run out. Such systems are available for 12 and 24 volt supply, and are commonly used to provide for two or three basins and a shower, although supply becomes increasingly erratic as the number of outlets increases.

Water heaters are usually of three types: the wall-mounted gas heater or geyser; heating pipes incorporated in a liquid fuel heater or cooker; or a 'calorifier' using waste heat from the engine. Wall heaters suitable for bottled gas are available for either single or multiple outlet systems, with provision for adjustment, and, most important, a flame failure device. An outlet flue is necessary. Liquid fuel heaters, mentioned elsewhere, are complex and require liaison with the manufacturers. Calorifiers come 'off the shelf' from such companies as the G. & M. Power Plant Co. of Ipswich, or the Stone Boat Building Co. of Stone, Staffordshire; but they can be made up by a number of concerns. In principle, the calorifier is a simple heat exchanger, a water tank of aluminium, stainless steel or copper through which passes a hot water pipe from the engine. Some may be adapted to electric heating as well, but this is beyond the capacity of most small craft systems. Two important points with all such water heating and storage installations are the need for good insulation, with heavy lagging over all exposed surfaces, and especially provision for expansion. A relief or safety valve is absolutely essential.

Electrical pumping is now common for draining shower trays, sometimes with a flotation switch, often with a pushbutton for draining the tray as it fills, hopefully arranged to minimize the risk of short-circuiting through damp.

All such pumps need to be protected from blocking, and bilge pumps in particular need a strum, or strainer, to prevent wood shavings, hair, matchsticks and other litter from clogging the inlet in a crisis. If none is provided, a simple strum box can often be made from an old milk tin, or similar, punched with a spike to make a sieve, then pushed onto the pump hose or held in place with a Jubilee (hose) clip. Bilge pumps driven by belt from the main engine are sometimes fitted instead and are often held to be the more reliable, although the hand-operated type is even more foolproof, and a bucket the most effective means of all.

Sewage

In Britain, more passion and discussion is generated by lavatorial matters on canals and rivers than the political future and continued uncertainty that surrounds the waterways themselves. There is now widespread legislation against emptying sewage into the navigation, although it is not always clear what happens at the emptying points provided by the authorities, or what becomes of the chemical that is so often added.

Flushing or pump-through yacht 'toilets' are therefore *infra dig* (and so too, on waterways such as the upper Thames, are sinks emptying into the stream) unless they are connected to a holding tank. If so used, they are best arranged to flush with fresh water, with no chemical additive, and with frequent emptying will be less likely to clog. Some electrically pumped units are available, while a small 'macerator' pump is available from ITT Fluid Handling, who also provide diagrams for plumbing circuitry. Pumps of this type are intended for intermittent operation only.

Sewage pump-out on the Norfolk Broads.

Problems with pump-through WCs are:

1. Blocking – sometimes overcome by filling to a higher level with fresh water, and then pumping; failing that, inserting a hose into the bowl, and by means of a hand pump sucking back the obstruction. Failing that, dismantling.

2. Fracture of components – some units are somewhat flimsy, not only in the linkages, but in the mounting of the bowl itself.

Problems with holding tanks are:

1. Failure of the emptying pump, if installed on board. Spares or an alternative hand pumping system are advised. On inland waterways, however, pump-out stations will do the job – provided that a standard access pipe is installed.

2. Clogging of the tank itself, through adding chemical or infrequent emptying. The ideal tank is said to be V-bottomed but with all edges rounded, sloping, and with a bolt-on inspection cover big enough to get a shovel through.

3. Lack of an emptying station – an important point to verify. Some sanitary stations are for chemical containers only, carried ashore by hand. Others have full pumping-out installations, while a number of hire companies maintain facilities at their own bases, and aim to install holding tanks that are big enough to survive until a boat next returns.

A simple alternative is the chemical privy, which if the worst comes to the worst can be emptied into a hole dug in waste ground. The simplest are merely a bucket, usually of plastic, with a seat and a cover, and these are charged before use with a little water and a measured quantity of chemical fluid. More elaborate flushing or recirculating types are now obtainable. These shield the users from the realities of the operation – save the person who does the emptying, who is often faced with a complicated and sordid range of connections. They have the disadvantage of reduced capacity, because of the volume taken by fresh water used for flushing; but daily emptying is really a necessity with all bucket-type containers, certainly in hot weather.

Steering systems

The simple tiller is the most precise. Those on motor narrow boats are traditionally secured in place by a pin with a brass head (usually a bed knob) and demounted when not in use. Modern tillers tend to be too light and whippy; the sturdier the better, and a tilted mounting, or a balanced rudder, with part of its area forward of the stock or pivot point, will be less likely to slam over when going astern. The length should be such that the tiller will not strike the wall when entering a lock, and if the end is made of wood, it will be comfortable on chilly days.

Wheels permit such luxuries as sitting down. Barge wheels are mounted on a heavy cogwheel system, the gipsy, through which a chain passes. The chain in turn connects to a quadrant above the rudder, sometimes directly, more often by means of wire cables running through pulleys. Wear in the gipsy cogs or slack cables both make steering harder, and more irritating. Small boat systems, similar in principle, often suffer from the same fault. Turnbuckle tensioners help, so does regular greasing of wires and pulleys.

Push-pull cable systems are available for small boats; also hydraulic steering systems, as well as rotating rods with universal couplings. The first of these is the most common on inland waterways, and is comparatively easy to install, with a single cable working an arm attached to the rudder stock. Alternative holes in the arm permit a choice of gearing – a subtly important factor in all wheel systems. Hydraulic systems are expensive, but permit dual installation, working from a pump at each steering position and a ram at the rudder. There is usually a loss of 'feel'. In theory they require no maintenance, but all wheel systems are vulnerable to failure: through chains or wires slipping or jamming, pins and linkages dropping out, air leaks, etc. A squared end on top of the rudder stock, and an emergency tiller to fit on it, are a worthwhile standby.

For outboards and outdrives, simple bolt-on rudder attachments are available, and these can improve handling at low speeds, or with the engine in neutral.

Buoyancy aids and life-rings

To wear or not to wear? It is easy to urge the wearing of 'life-jackets' at all times; not so easy to follow the dictum oneself. Try it in the heat, when in and out of the cabin every five

137

minutes, when having to put on other clothing, and so on. Only the diligent persist.

Fully-fledged life-jackets should provide at least 35 lb buoyancy and they are correspondingly bulky. A British Standard has been devised, with appropriate 'kitemark' stamping for approved devices. Compromise 'buoyancy aids' are also available, and may be earnestly recommended for children (especially if they go off on their own), non-swimmers (particularly, but not exclusively, on wider rivers), and for the generally safety-conscious. There is a variety of types, employing permanent buoyancy, inflatability, or a combination. Some are like waistcoats; others are placed over the head, then secured around the waist with line. The Ship and Boat Builders' National Federation has set standards, verified by the mark 'SBBNF Approved'.

Such aids should enable the wearer to float upright, but with the shoulders back. Minimum buoyancy necessary is said to be 18 lb for someone weighing 140 lbs, and less for lighter bodies. In practice children require proportionately more buoyancy, and should really be given as much as possible, but the garment must not float up around the head when in the water. Those with permanent buoyancy stitched in are the more foolproof – some have foam, others plastic sachets – but they are bulky. Inflatable types can be neat and compact, but depend on mouth inflation in the water, or the wearer triggering a small gas bottle. The latter type will tolerate a small degree of mouth inflation first, and can be deflated again by using a plastic prodder down the nozzle. It is very easy to forget this, and to leave the nozzle in the 'deflation' condition next time the device is worn.

In the past, various safety garments have appeared with ingenious but doubtful devices, such as fabrics that seal when wet, chemical interaction to produce gas, etc. Beware of them.

All buoyancy garments need careful maintenance, with cleaning, rinsing if contaminated in any way, and periodic checking for tears, worn stitching, porosity etc. Life-rings or life-buoys are preferably light (but not too light) and uncluttered by lanyards, drogues, lights etc, at least for inland use. The type shaped like a horseshoe is easier to struggle into. Inflatable rings, plastic ducks and so on will be difficult to throw and are more likely to blow away.

Trailers

There are many types on the market and kits are also available. Attributes are sturdiness, plenty of reserve in the suspension, and adequate support for the boat over as great a length as possible. The choice is often between chocks and rollers, but if the boat is flat-bottomed, or straight along the keel, long wooden slats will give a more even support, and if kept well greased will permit easy launching and recovery.

Trailing generates its own lore, and owners will sometimes tell hair-raising stories of the weights they can tow, and the rapidity of launching and recovery. Car suppliers should be consulted regarding suitable loads for a particular model (an 8 cwt total load for a 1000 cc car, 15 cwt for 1300 cc, 1 ton for 2000 cc, 2 tons for a 'Range Rover' are common recommendations). An approved towbar and coupling should always be fitted; the 50 mm ball hitch is now virtually standard, but 2 in fittings are still about and the two sizes should never be mixed. The law, despite ambiguities, is specific on certain points: to travel at 50 mph, the total weight of an unbraked trailer and load must not exceed 60 per cent of that of the towing vehicle, but over-run braking systems are mandatory for trailers exceeding 2 cwt unladen. Other requirements are an approved lighting board, from 1 ft 3 in to 3 ft 6 in above the road, with lights and red triangles within 1 ft 4 in of the extreme width, and a '50' maximum speed sign. All these should theoretically be on the trailer, but in practice are accepted on the boat herself. A seven-pin connecting socket is necessary, with provision for turning indicators, all wired in parallel to the car circuit, and the weight of the car and petrol, but minus passengers, should be marked on the vehicle's nearside.

If only 40 mph is to be attempted, some of these requirements can be overlooked, including weight ratio, but police may take action in cases of dangerous overloading. The width limit is 7 ft 6 in, and 7 metres the length, excluding drawbar in the majority of cases. Craft carrying an unprotected outboard have been queried; removal of the propeller, or covering it with pad-

139

ding and a bright reflective surface, appears to satisfy some authorities.

In towing, it pays to carry a spare wheel and to keep hub bearings well greased. If the trailer is to be immersed, greasing both before and after is advised. Beware of putting the trailer into water immediately after arrival, since the bearings should first be allowed to cool. When towing, balance can be critical; a 30–50 lb downward load at the hitch is an optimum. Loads need to be tied on firmly, against shifting on corners or during emergency braking. It is useful to mark the trailer clearly, particularly for towing *empty* in heavy traffic, when flagstaffs above the wheels have their merits.

The interior

Cabin divisions are usually of faced board, or occasionally of a timber framework covered in plywood or hardboard panels. Sound insulation is usually negligible, and is difficult to achieve without using very dense materials sealed round at every edge. Certain types of household partitioning using plasterboard sandwich or a honeycomb core, have reasonable sound-insulating qualities, but the slightest gap at the edge will nullify the effort. Almost without exception, boatbuilders have abandoned this unequal struggle, and merely use plywood, or board faced with a laminate.

Engine installations can sometimes be quietened by close-fitting hatches and surroundings of heavy material, but such work is difficult and expensive. Foam, acoustic boarding, and other panaceas have a regrettably small effect.

Condensation and ventilation go hand in hand, but insulation can help considerably. Polystyrene foam is sometimes used, but is a fire risk, likewise some of the foam-backed materials sold. Hessian, or an anti-condensation paint such as Korkon (produced by International Paints), will sometimes do the trick, but thick wooden boarding is often the most effective.

Ventilators come in an infinity of shapes and sizes. For inland waterways they do not need to be proof against waves splashing on board, but there is rain and roof-washing to consider, so some sort of trap is desirable. An effective type is shaped like a flying saucer, perforated around the rim and with a flange inside to keep the water out. A further important advantage is outside smoothness, which makes it unlikely to catch ropes – a point that applies to all outside fittings, and particularly to handrails, where the ends should not project.

Windows have been the bugbear of boatbuilders in the past, because of their complexity (and uncertain delivery), but greater standardization on waterways craft has brought ease of installation and reliability. There is no necessity for heavily sealed and armoured portlights of the seagoing kind, and the areas used may be large without fear of being stove in. Louvre-opening windows tend to catch the knees of those passing, however, and the swing-open type can be swept away in locks; a common design nowadays has a small hopper opening at the top and a fixed pane below. Sliding types tend to be more expensive, but there is such a wide variety in pricing that it pays to obtain alternative quotations. Canal boat windows often have an anodized aluminium frame with an overlapping outside flange. Fixing can be with screws, bolts, or pop-rivets, with the frame edge bedded onto a layer of *non-hardening* mastic.

Mattresses

Thickness is a common, but misleading, criterion. There are thousands of different kinds of foam, and terms such as 'high density' can mean very little. Resilience and recovery rate can be judged by sitting or lying, and there is no substitute for personal sampling.

Boat mattresses are usually vinyl covered, to resist the inevitable damp, and can be made up by a number of firms, to any reasonable size, or from paper patterns. If making up a mattress oneself, it is important to make covers oversize, with an extra $\frac{3}{4}$ in at each edge. Cotton 'rep' is a reasonably suitable material, but any fabric other than vinyl should theoretically be laid on a ventilated support, ideally a woven net. In practice, laying it upon plywood, with frequent lifting for ventilation and some air holes, will give a reasonable life.

Rope

Artificial fibres now give a blessed freedom from rot, and great strength and reliability. For inland use, types that are kind to the hands and do not stretch unduly are the most favoured. This rules out nylon (stretchy), which is also expensive and tends to fray; and for many, orange Courlene (polythene), which is hard, unsympathetic, slippery and difficult to knot.

Most other types are suitable; polyester is often used, under the generic trade name Terylene or Dacron, as well as other names. Polypropylene, cheaper and widely sold under various trade names, is lightweight, floats, strong, and convenient to handle. It is difficult to be precise about sizes and loadings, but a well-found vessel will have at least two mooring warps of 35–40 ft each, and one of 60 ft, each with an eye splice at one end. This may seem excessive, but lock walls can be high, as much for small craft as for large. On Continental waterways, two 60 ft ropes will be necessary for mooring, and it is handy to have another as a spare. For a heavy vessel, such as a 70 ft narrow boat, or similar, polyester with a $2\frac{1}{2}$ in circumference (20 mm diameter) will be sufficient, but some prefer 3 in to be on the safe side. Small light craft, such as 25 ft fibreglass cruisers, can manage with $1\frac{3}{4}$ in polyester (14 mm diameter) and arguably less, although the thinner the rope, the more self-tangling and difficult to manage it becomes.

Ropes are often stored in coils, with the end wound around, but this can result in a tangle, and common seagoing practice is to tie big coils with light cotton in two or three places, simply snapping it free when needed.

The ends of artificial fibre rope are often flame-sealed, a

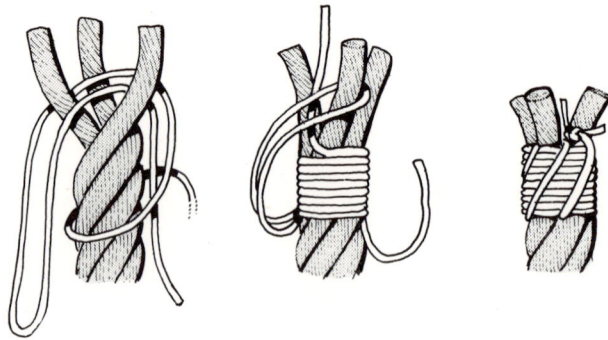

Whipping a rope's end. A loop of twine is first laid between the strands, before winding the rest round, pulling tight and knotting the ends.

slightly hazardous performance, best tackled by heating cautiously in the fringes of a gas ring, and pressing with a knife, or metal foil, held in a cloth. Such ends often come unstuck, and a simple whipping with artificial fibre twine is more satisfactory. There are many types, but one of the most successful is made by laying a loop around one of the strands, winding the rest of the twine around the rope above it, and dropping the end of the loop back over the same strand. The outstanding ends are then drawn together and knotted. A good whipping should theoretically be no longer than the diameter of the rope, but has to be as tight as possible to avoid being pulled off.

Fenders, buckets, shafts and flags

Those with a nautical bent consider it slovenly to travel with fenders dangling, although fragile boats may need them so often that the performance of raising and lowering becomes quite ludicrous. In such cases it is better to risk ridicule and keep them hanging. But the best inland boats do not need them – save on the bow and very occasionally at the stern.

Bow fenders are important for all craft, to protect lock gates and other vessels from being harpooned. Many canal boat fenders are of woven rope, and may be bought at waterside shops or yards. Those wishing to make their own will find references in *Ashley's Book of Knots* – a monumental work. The bigger a bow fender the better, and boats with a long vertical stem may need several, hung one above another. Each should be woven around a chain, as the most durable and chafe-resistant method of attachment. Craft of the narrow boat type traditionally have another fender, or rather a group of them, laid one upon another, to hang on the stern and protect the rudder.

Fenders on the side of the hull can be awkward. The plastic type gets swept aside, or jammed behind lock gates when entering, while rope will do the same and also chafe. Motor tyres are crude but more effective. They are best secured with wire or chain, but tough rope may suffice, threaded through two holes, bored in a non-chafing position with a brace-and-bit. A further hole at the bottom will permit water collected inside to drain away. For very heavy steel boats, hardwood blocks or strips hanging vertically on a wire will take hard punishment when flexible fenders would simply crush, and they can be useful in absorbing the shock if swept across a lock. For most practical purposes, however, a heavy metal boat can manage without.

Buckets cheerily painted with roses are traditional on the narrow canals. The time-honoured position is just forward of the cabin chimney on the port (left hand) side. The mop end rests on the handle, within the steerer's reach. Cans may be bought ready-painted, or home-decorated in the manner described earlier. If used for drinking water, it might be an idea to leave the rim of the spout unpainted.

Shafts or poles must obviously be strong, not too whippy, and of some straight-grained wood such as spruce. While a very short boathook is occasionally useful, there is little necessity for long shafts to carry any hook or spike at all. Shafts up to 18 ft can be useful in poling off shallows, or poking around the bottom, provided there is room to stow them. A diameter of $2\frac{1}{2}$ in should just be manageable. Some enthusiasts paint them in stripes, which not only look jolly but can be useful in gauging depth if, say, the colours change at every foot in length. When long poles get old they often start to break up, tearing at the grain, to yield a host of nasty splinters. Varnishing and sanding may work temporarily, but they should really be thrown away. For large vessels such as barges, or over-sized boats prone to sticking in locks, they may be fitted with a rake end instead, for hooking out stones or bricks lodged behind the gates.

Flags have volumes written about them, and the pitfalls are legion. Their care is easy enough: the less a flag is exposed to the weather, the longer it will last, provided it is not put away wet. Since flags cannot be seen at night, they may be stored for that period. Someone in the Navy long ago decreed when night should end and begin: at 8 am in summer, 9 am in winter, and concluding at 'sunset', as officially listed in almanacs and diaries. More elaborate ceremonials are occasionally explored by boating clubs, in which all manner of ensigns and bunting are flown, dipped, saluted, and so on.

For the ordinary user, much of this can be ignored. The Red Ensign, the flag of the Merchant Navy, is the correct one for most Britons to fly from the stern of their craft – not the 'Union Jack' (really called the Union Flag); not the Blue Ensign, unless on behalf of a Government department, or personally warranted by certain clubs; certainly not the White Ensign (unless Royal Navy or a member of the Royal Yacht Squadron at Cowes).

Club and Association burgees can be flown at the masthead if there is one, but a flag at the bow is most useful in judging distance in locks, or warning oncomers at a bend. This is common practice on Continental barges, which often fly great banners in rivers and estuaries (up high, so they may be seen above lock gates and approach walls), and at all times a great medley of International flags and pennants. Similar practices might bring more colour and bonhomie to home rivers and canals, but if devising a personal emblem, take care that it does not symbolize Lithuania, 'I require a pilot', or 'conducting a speed trial'.

The Law and Insurance

BY A LAWYER

When one takes a car on the road it must be licensed and insured and it must, in its construction, conform to the Construction and Use Regulations. It must be driven only by a
qualified person who has passed the Driving Test. Generally
speaking, life on the water is free of these restrictions. There
is no national system for licensing boats and, though the folly
of not being insured should be obvious, there is no legal obligation to obtain cover for the damage you may cause in navigating
a boat. However, for most inland waterways the controlling
authority imposes its own licensing requirements so that there
is, in fact, a piecemeal system of control on the use of boats.

A river or canal authority, or the authority controlling a lake,
may therefore oblige you to pay an annual registration fee and,
as a condition of granting use of the waterway in question, may
oblige a boat to be built and equipped to adequate standards.
On canals, at any rate, there may be an obligation imposed
that the vessel be adequately insured. Byelaw offences may be
committed if requirements are not complied with and, of
course, a mass of byelaws exist to control speed limits, mooring,
noise, pollution, navigation, and so on upon particular waterways. Local enquiry should therefore always be made.

Collision is the kind of mishap on inland waterways which
is most likely to involve costly repair bills and, if it should come
to court proceedings, all the circumstances are considered.
Negligence has to be proved by a claimant, namely, a falling

below a reasonable standard of careful navigation. He must prove this on a balance of probabilities and he may be met by the defence that what occurred was a pure accident or that he himself was wholly or in part to blame. If both parties are at fault and it proves impossible to assess degrees of fault a judge or arbitrator would usually say that the loss is to be borne equally.

The International Collision Regulations apply to the high seas and 'all waters connected therewith navigable by seagoing vessels' unless there are local rules to the contrary. Local rules in fact apply to a great number of our waterways and, on lakes, you may find rules for navigation made under the Countryside Acts or the National Parks legislation. Indeed, if no local rules have actually been promulgated a court would then probably ask what were the customary rules for navigation generally accepted in that area and would consider that a departure from these could be held to be evidence of negligence. Again one sees the importance of local enquiry.

Insurance

It is imperative to carry adequate insurance against injury or damage to other people or their property. Certainly on the canal system, the British Waterways Board has legal power to compel you to carry insurance because, as owners of the actual beds and banks of these artificial waterways, they can impose what conditions they like on those given leave to enter their property. On river waterway navigations this power probably does not as yet exist and, when you apply for registration under the British Waterways Act 1971, the carrying of insurance is not a prerequisite to the grant of the Certificate. The distinction is illogical because the risk of accidents where third party cover would be useful is probably greater on rivers than on canals.

As to hired craft, the British Waterways Board has a fleet of these and arranges insurance to cover themselves but not the risk carried by the hirer of the craft. About 10% of vessels on the canals are hire cruisers and 90% private craft. At present some 56% of all boats on canals do have comprehensive insurance and 6% have third party insurance at least.

Faced with ever rising costs, a boat owner may ask if savings

147

can be made in insurance premiums. One course is to increase the 'excess' in your policy, because general running costs are so high that there is little point in being insured for very minor claims. Remember, by the way, that if you do have a heavy loss and make a claim, the 'excess' is still applicable, so do not set it uncomfortably high. Cutting the insurance value of your boat will not save as much as you think, and of course if you suffer a total loss only the insured value will be paid out.

There are usually three main cruising areas specified in a policy, here listed in descending order of cost. First, full sea-going cruising between Brest and the Elbe with, in some policies, the inclusion of Continental waterways as far south as Paris. Do check. Otherwise you may not be covered once you enter a lock on the other side of the Channel. Second, coastal cruising within 10 miles of home port or permanent moorings. Third, non-tidal waters of the UK. All policies should cover the boat while stored within the UK.

It should go without saying that any unusual risks which you are intending to incur should be properly insured and declared to the insurers. You should particularly note that cruising through the inland waterways of Europe is not *automatically* covered in most policies, and therefore needs special mention. You will not necessarily be charged extra premium.

Cover in general

If you look at a standard form of marine insurance policy you will notice that the violence of man seems to be as prominent as a risk as the hazards of the elements. Fire was added only in modern times. Special clauses for yachts called the 'Institute Yacht Clauses' have been in use since 1926. But no insurer is obliged to use any particular 'standard' or 'official' policy, and many insurance companies will have their own form of Yacht or Motor Boat or Dinghy Policy which will have just a family resemblance to the big yacht policies used by Lloyds under-writers, carrying Institute Yacht Clauses.

Most policies will presuppose that the boat is in use for pleasure purposes only and will have three main heads of risk covered. (*1*) Loss of, or damage to, the boat by marine perils up to the value insured. This will cover such things as sinking, going aground, fire, collision, theft of the vessel and, following forcible entry, theft of the equipment and fittings. Remember that personal effects such as cameras, sleeping bags, etc are not usually included unless specially arranged. (2) Collision with other craft and loss or injury suffered by other people for which a legal liability may arise through the navigation of your boat. This includes damage to locks, piers, jetties, and so on. Removal of wreck is also included. This is your obligation to pay a water or harbour authority if it has to remove your foundered vessel. Your possible liability for injury to people on your own boat in an accident may well *not* be covered. Read the policy carefully. (3) Salvage charges claimed by salvors. Reasonable charges for preventing loss are likely to be paid under most policies, but, like much in insurance, this is a cloudy area. People sometimes think that salvage claims can only arise for services given at sea, but if a vessel is of a type and size to be fairly described as 'used in navigation' (not, say, a small dinghy or a houseboat) and is voluntarily rescued from a situation where it is in real danger of being lost, then a salvage claim can be made if it is successfully rescued. Obviously such a situation would be exceptional in inland waters.

Many policies will cover slipway risks, and insurance normally also covers land transport on a trailer (possibly with a provision for a maximum total length of, say, 20 ft) save in so far as risks are covered, or ought to be covered, by the usual Road Traffic Act car policy. So, if you trail to inland waters the boat is probably covered by the car policy until it is detached for launching, and then, even though still on the trailer, it is under your marine policy. In the event of accidental detachment while driving it will therefore be the car policy which covers your third party liability. Do inform your insurance company if you are in the habit of trailing.

'Fire risks' also covers explosions and the effects of lightning, and losses caused by actions taken in anticipation of, or in preventing, the spread of a fire have been accepted as proper claims. The loss, of course, must be accidental, but once you show a *prima facie* loss by a fire, then it would be for the insurance company to prove, if it could, that on a balance of probabilities the cause was deliberately caused or connived at by the owner.

Theft and wilful damage

The usual cover is against loss caused by someone who is not a member of the policyholder's family. If the loss arises other than within the area of a recognized boat club you will probably find that the cover extends (except for theft of the entire boat) only to equipment which is locked up, or locked to the boat, and outboards must be attached by means of a lock. 'Forcible entry' are vital words. Simple theft of gear left lying about is not covered in most marine policies. You may be doubtful of the strength of a small padlock, but proof that it was in use may be crucial in getting a claim allowed.

When a boat is lent

The practice of insurance companies varies here and it is most important to check that if you lend or hire out your own boat the cover remains operative. The owner's liability for accidents caused when someone else is at the helm of his boat essentially depends on right of control and is analogous to the position with motor vehicles.

First, there is the difference between a servant and an independent contractor. If you employ a helmsman you are liable for all his acts 'in the course of his employment in those duties'. If, however, a boatyard is, perhaps, test running your boat and causes damage by negligent navigation, then it is an independent contractor and you would not be liable. Incidentally, your policy will probably exclude from cover employees of boatyards injured when navigating or working on your boat, and it is their own employers who have to insure this risk with an Employer's Liability Policy. The boatyard will no doubt have done this, but do also note that most yards will not insure your boat while it is on the premises. Check that your own cover remains operative here, as damage can very easily occur to a boat while it is laid up ashore.

If you are on board your boat and allow your crew to helm, then you are probably liable in law if he is negligent. This is because you, as owner, are in overall control. He, of course, is also liable for his acts, but the party making the claim might well decide to seek his legal remedy only against the – probably – more prosperous owner. However, if you lent the boat, or hired it, to someone else for a weekend then he is using it simply for his own purposes and liability for what he may do would not be visited on you personally.

A caution should, however, be noted. It is a peculiarity of sea law that claims can be made against a vessel as well as against its owner. A court judgment *in rem* (against 'the thing') could be secured so that, if the judgment is unsatisfied, the boat itself could be ordered to be sold to meet the claim. Further, in a situation where a charterer, or borrower, exposes the vessel to a claim, arising for example from collision with harbour works or another vessel, or as a result of salvage services being given to it, not only could a claim arise against the vessel itself, but unless financial security was forthcoming, it might be lawfully detained under a 'lien' pending settlement of the dispute. Borrowers and charterers should be most carefully selected, and if your insurance company agrees that you may charter, it will probably insist that it will not be liable for any failure by the hirer to comply with his charter agreement.

Third party liability

The likely absence of cover for your liability to third parties who may be on your boat has already been noted. Certainly you could incur such a liability. Most owners have to tolerate ineptitude. In a law case some twenty years ago an owner fitting out on the Thames accepted a friend's help with a blowlamp near an empty petrol tank. The resulting explosion when fumes leaked through the unstopped filler hole blew up the boat and injured the friend. He alleged negligence by the owner, namely, failure to warn him of the situation. In a cross claim the owner claimed for loss of his boat, saying that the friend had had adequate warning and had, by his negligence in putting the blowlamp near the hole, destroyed the boat. The court found that the owner had indeed given full warning to the 'volunteer' and the latter had to pay damages for the loss of the craft. However, it might well have been otherwise and then the owner would have had to read his insurance policy in the hope that it had cover for all claims by third parties 'for which the assured is legally liable'.

The more likely third party risk is of course that your boat will cause injury or loss by collision with another vessel or with locks, landing stages, etc. You can be visited with liability for damage to various harbour works under statutes which impose the liability 'absolutely', i.e. whether or not you have been negligent. If you collide with another vessel and so force her to cause damage to a third vessel, the legal damages she may have to pay the third vessel, and could therefore recover in a claim against you, are also within the cover you get under collision risk. Insurance companies do not normally accept liability to cover a vessel when it is being used as a towing vessel or for water skiing or for towing objects other than boats. Special rates will be quoted for these risks.

Limitation of liability

How much cover do you need for third party risks? Sometimes the third party indemnity is equal to the figure for which the boat is itself insured. This is normally entirely inadequate, and many insurers are increasing the third party cover they give you as a matter of course. Even these increases could be inadequate. Under marine law, which extends to all water used by vessels engaged 'in navigation', there is power to limit one's liability when one's vessel causes injury or damage. This is not confined to the high seas but extends to inland waters connected to the sea because 'navigation' can occur in such waters. International agreement specifies a maximum liability in gold francs which, at the present value of sterling, comes to about £37 per ton for property damage and £106 per ton for personal injury or death. The tonnage is the registered tonnage of the offending vessel, and if it is not a registered vessel, it would have to be measured before it could claim to limit. Registration in this context means registration with the Dept. of Trade as a 'British Ship', and the great majority of small craft never go through the expensive process of such registration.

The effect is that if, say, a 5 ton cruiser negligently collides with another vessel and does perhaps £3000 of damage it can claim a maximum liability of not over 5 multiplied by £37 or £185. Serious injuries can be caused to persons in apparently safe waters. A waterskier, mangled by a screw, obtained judgment for £50,000 even fifteen years ago. So, to obviate

152

hardship to such victims, a minimum platform tonnage of 300 tons is used for 'limitation' situations where damages are awarded for injury or death. Hence the limit here for even the smallest vessel begins at 300 × 106 or £31,800. You cannot limit below this figure, and the wise owner has hitherto been insuring for at least £32,000 for possible liability for injury or death.

Limitation cuts both ways. If a reckless uninsured owner of a small launch causes your vessel, say, £1000 of damage he can probably limit his liability to 2 or 3 tons multiplied by £37. Unless you are insured you will have to meet the rest of your loss out of your own pocket – even though you may have been peacefully moored at the time of the accident and he admits he was totally to blame. He has used his marine right to limit.

Limitation can be claimed even if a vessel damages harbour works. The point is causing general anxiety to harbour authorities whose installations can now be very expensive to repair even when damaged by small craft. Further, a pleasure vessel might hit and damage, say, an oil rig and then be able to limit liability for this property damage to a few hundred pounds, or even less. Hence, there is now a strong probability that the position set out above will soon be altered.

A new Convention on Limitation of Liability has been signed by the United Kingdom as a result of an international conference in November 1976, and a new system of limitation under British law seems imminent. By this, uniform treatment of small craft 'limitation' claims would be secured, especially among European countries. The proposal is that a minimum tonnage will also apply to *property* claims, i.e. all small vessels will now be deemed to be of 500 tons for both property damage *and* injury claims, and the maximum claims will be fixed in units of account of a present sterling value of £111,890 and £223,110.

Insurance market enquiries show that insurance premiums for these much increased sums are unlikely to rise appreciably – possibly by only £10 per annum for the largest yachts.

One should add, in this crystal ball exercise, that there is a possibility that the coming legislation will in fact fix 300 and not 500 tons as the 'deemed' tonnage and in that case the maximum figures will be substantially less.

Exceptions

Several situations have already been referred to where your policy may well not provide cover. Some others which should be noted are:

where safety regulations have not been observed.

while the boat is being used to earn money, unless special arrangements are made.

if damage is caused deliberately or through gross negligence.

if the boat is not properly equipped, or is carelessly launched.

the loss of an outboard motor dropping overboard.

damage caused by or consisting of faulty construction or materials, or lack of seaworthiness.

no payments will be made for loss of time or other indirect loss.

The insured has a general duty of care. This is not easy to define with precision, but is referred to in most policies as 'lack of due diligence'. It is reasonable for an insurance company to anticipate that you will be as diligent as possible in protecting and managing your property. It is not, as a lot of people think, sufficient to say: 'Oh, leave it there, it's insured!' or, to take another example, to allow your boat to drift onto a weir merely because you have been so lacking in 'due diligence' as to try to sail on an unknown river without an engine.

The measure of compensation

If one boat owner negligently damages the craft of another, the object of the damages which have to be negotiated, or assessed by a court, will be to place the owner of the lost or damaged vessel as nearly as may be in the same position as he would have been but for the collision. If yours is the boat that is damaged you have an obligation to make all reasonable efforts to minimize the loss, e.g. by trying to prevent her from sinking. You must not refuse reasonable offers of help or unreasonably abandon her.

If a vessel is totally lost the owner should recover her value. In most cases this is market value, and if she suffers a constructive total loss (see below) he can recover her value as if she were actually and totally lost. When the vessel is not lost but damaged, the owner will be entitled to reasonable cost of repairs and to such expenses as salvage and towing charges, and survey fees. He is entitled to the cost of repairs even though, as in the case of the renewal of sails, the end result may be an improvement in the condition and value of the vessel by the substitution of new for old materials. The cost of temporary as well as the permanent repairs can also sometimes be recovered. It may depend on the efficiency of your solicitor!

When a boat is out of use a holiday may be spoiled. As it is not a vessel used for profit the measurement of the loss here may present problems. But inconvenience and loss of pleasure is something for which legal damages can be claimed. If there was a clear demand for the boat for chartering then the problem is lessened: a yardstick exists. A yacht maintained solely for letting on the Broads had damages calculated this way some years ago. An alternative is to assess the capital value of the boat and claim loss of interest on this sum while repairs delay your use of the asset. If you have to hire another boat of equivalent type while yours is under repair you could claim this expense. The whole matter is rather open to negotiation.

Loss when helping someone in distress

Reverting to insurance, one should note that under the normal policy there will be no cover for loss of life or personal accident which occurs to the insured himself. He will therefore get nothing if he suffers injury or is drowned in the course of a rescue operation. Subject to this, however, most reputable companies will cover loss and damage to your boat arising while it is engaged in a rescue operation, provided it has not resulted from a lack of 'due diligence' by those in charge of the rescuing boat. The fact that you respond to a call for help, or even take the initiative yourself, would not defeat your claim unless it could clearly be held that either the character of your boat or your own inexperience made the rescue attempt completely foolhardy.

When loss occurs

You must at once inform the insurers when loss or damage occurs. If you are rescued from a position of danger do not make any agreement with salvors as to fees without first consulting the insurance company. If the damage is to your vessel the company is entitled to say where it is to be repaired and to ask you to get tenders, but the cost of allowable repairs need not necessarily be the lowest tender because the standard you are entitled to demand is ascertained by looking at the general condition of your boat. If repairs are unduly deferred and costs rise the company is probably not liable for the difference.

Your boat could be a total loss. This may be actual or constructive. The latter idea is peculiar to marine law and occurs when you reasonably abandon the boat because repairs would cost so much that they would exceed its value when repaired. You can, in such a case, give 'notice of abandonment' and treat the loss as total. The test is, what would a prudent uninsured owner do about his boat if it was damaged to this degree – would he try to sell her as she lies or repair her?

You cannot add the cost of repairs to the value of the wreck to get the total sum which is to be compared to the repaired value. Therefore, if a boat is insured for £3000 and suffers loss which will cost £2900 to repair, you cannot make a constructive total loss claim, but if the repairs will cost £3100 such a claim does arise. The company may of course refuse to accept your notice of abandonment and contest whether it was justified. Temporary and subsequent complete repairs may be totalled in estimating 'cost of repairs'.

The right to navigate

These notes have mainly referred to waterways. Rivers and lakes are, in the eyes of the law, simply areas of water covering private land. However, on most of our larger rivers there is a public right of navigation. This is a right to pass and repass and to anchor for a reasonable time. On a tidal river or creek, on the other hand, there is, as well as the right to navigate, also a right to fish. As for putting down moorings, there is no general right to do this either in fresh water or tidal water. This will involve trespass to land owned by somebody – probably the Crown or a long leaseholder from the Crown, such as a local authority, in the case of tidal waters. Remember also that one may not go ashore from a waterway or moor up against its bank just anywhere.

Towpaths of course are open to the public, but to a limited degree. There is usually no legal right to drive on them with vehicles like cars or motorcycles. Activities like camping are likely to be legally obstructions in strict law, and the right to use a towpath does not in itself give any right to take a rod and line there.

Index